The
Humanistic Approach
in
Psychology & Psychotherapy,
Sociology & Social Work,
Pedagogy & Education,
Management and Art:

*Personal Development
and
Community Development*

The Humanistic Approach in Psychology & Psychotherapy, Sociology & Social Work, Pedagogy & Education, Management and Art:

Personal Development and Community Development

Author:
Petru Stefaroi

Cover:
Ionut Platon, Petru Stefaroi

ISBN-13: 978-1535271646
ISBN-10: 1535271647

CreateSpace, Charleston SC, an Amazon.com Company
4900 LaCross Road, North Charleston, SC 29406, USA

Includes Bibliography

Paperback: 198 pages

Product Dimensions: 5,5" x 8,5" / 13.97 x 21.59 cm

THE
HUMANISTIC
APPROACH

in

Psychology & Psychotherapy, Sociology & Social Work, Pedagogy & Education, Management and Art

*Personal Development
and Community Development*

by Petru Stefaroi

The
Humanistic Approach
in
Psychology & Psychotherapy,
Sociology & Social Work,
Pedagogy & Education,
Management and Art:

*Personal Development
and
Community Development*

"Life
is not a Problem
to be Solved,
but a Reality
to be Experienced."

Søren Kierkegaard

"Man is the Measure of All Things"

\- **Protagoras** \-

TABLE OF CONTENTS

The
Humanistic Approach
in
Psychology & Psychotherapy,
Sociology & Social Work,
Pedagogy & Education,
Management and Art:

Personal Development
and
Community Development

CONTENTS

The
Humanistic Approach
in
Psychology & Psychotherapy,
Sociology & Social Work,
Pedagogy & Education,
Management and Art:

*Personal Development
and
Community Development*

INTRODUCTION

In this book is made a brief presentation of the main orientations and features of the *humanistic* theory and method in the major socio-human sciences, domains, and practices.

As construction, structure and content this book cumulates, incorporates, synthesizes and develops in a new, original and unitary work a number of our previous works consecrated to the humanistic approach and method in some socio-human sciences and practices, especially in psychology and psychotherapy, sociology, social work, education and management, published up to the end of 2012, both in print and electronic format.

It's, therefore, about works (articles and books) as *"Humanistic Orientation in the Social Sciences and Practices"*; *"Empathy and Compathy in the Social Relationships and Groups*; *"Humanistic Sociology"*; *"Humanistic Psychology and Humanistic Social Work"*; *"Humanistic Social Work Theories and Methods: Personality – Core Resource of Practice"*; *"Humanistic Paradigm of Social Work or Brief Introduction in Humanistic Social Work"*; *"Humanistic Perspective on Customer in Social Work"*; *"Happiness Theory in Social Work. From Care Management to Happiness Management"*; *"Socio-Affective Development Disorders of Institutionalized Child. From The Survival Objective towards the Happiness Objective in Social Work for Children"*; *"Efficient Management Particularity in Social Work"* (some titles are translated from Romanian).

Both in the realization of the works mentioned above as well of the present book was taken into consideration and was consulted the universal "social" and "therapeutic" literature of humanistic orientation (with the two main directions – *existential/positive* and *spiritual/humanitarian*) or the one that describe them or refer to them.

Essentially, the **Humanistic-Existential (Positive) Orientation/ Theory** represents the ***person*** and ***personality*** through *traits* like high level of personal and social autonomy, free will and high capacity/ ability to self-determination, high level of personal development, high resilience, high capacity to control the emotions, high degree of awareness, self-knowledge, high self-esteem, high level of interpersonal development, adaptability, mature personality, activism and initiative, assertiveness, etc., while the **socio-human (micro-)community** is represented through *features* such as high autonomy, strong organizational culture, high socio-human functionality, high cohesion, unity, solidity, adaptability, resilience, resistance to crisis and challenges, good management, etc.

The humanistic-existential approaches promote core concepts as *strong personality* and *strong community, personal development* and *community development.*

As value-objective of practice **strong personality** and **strong microcommunity** applied to the field of humanistic psycho-therapy and education, to humanistic social work and humanistic management help to a better understanding of the relationships between the client/ student/ employee and the living environment/ organization, representing them by traits like high socio-human functionality, durability, consistency, etc.

In psychotherapy the humanistic-existential paradigm of the client, originated in existential and positive (phenomenological) philosophy, determines the focalization of intervention on **personal development** and social adjustment through using the psycho-volitional and intellectual-adaptive means/ resources, highlighting, therefore, its phenomenological-contextual and psychological-adaptive dimensions, the responsibility, the free will, the freedom and capacity of the person/ client to overcome with its own resources the situation of difficulty.

To this end, one of the most important aim of the psychotherapy is to contribute to the development of psychological-personal and social-behavioral traits and qualities such as self-control, consciousness, activism, self-determination, optimism, energy, free will, self-realization, personal development, social and cultural adaptability, sociality, social implication, assertiveness, resilience, happiness, etc.

The Humanistic-Spiritual/ Humanitarian Approaches/ Theories promote as core concepts *spiritual-humane personality* and *humane/good community, spiritual-humane development* of the person and *humane-cultural development of the community.*

Representing the **person** and **personality (spiritual-humane personality)** it highlights especially the inner-ontological psychological-spiritual and psychological-humane content/ valence/ dimensions, spirituality, virtue, humanity, the spiritual and humane self. This paradigm gives so to the ontological-spiritual and psychological-humane sphere the primary etiological and structural role in formation, structure, and functioning of the person/ personality. It highlights and promotes *personality traits and qualities* such as spirituality, virtue, humanness, altruism, empathy, love, faith, etc.

Regarding the theoretical representation of the **community (humane/ good community)** this approach/ theory highlights *ideas* and *features* as people-centered community, the dominance of the inter-personal relationships of attachment, love, respect, the dominance of the practices and customs of mutual helps, social/ group/ community solidarity, harmony, unity, inter-personal congruency, socio-human, inter-personal, community functionality, socio-human, moral and cultural integration/ cohesion, the presence/ dominance of people with personality and behavioral traits like altruism, empathy, kindness, goodness, tolerance, understanding, helpfulness, etc.

In practice, regarding the person, this approach proposes and promotes the client's recovery through **spiritual and human/ humane development,** through (re-) spiritualization and humanization, starting from the representation of the person/ client's personality (as resource and objective) on the one hand as personality developed at higher level, the most high, the most close to the condition of human being as autonomous cultural, rational, spiritual existence, with its specific, characteristical attributes - morality, virtue, sociality, spirituality, humane development, adaptability and socio-human efficiency, and, on the other hand as personality structured through the self, ego, conscience, character, motivation, skills, etc. so that determines conducts oriented towards the wellbeing of the generalized other, towards the common good, humanity, and dominant traits such as empathy, altruism, generosity, kindness, humanness, etc.

Regarding the community, in practice, this approach proposes and promotes the community emancipation and recovery through **cultural, moral and humane development**, through the formation, establishment and development of a *humane, good community/ society*. In this kind of community, social group, organization each member is part of a compathetical/ humane system; the compathetical/ humane consistency being given especially by the fact that the individual personalities are composed of common experiences, by the fact that in each individual personality exists, through empathy and humanness, the others. Are established so a mutual existential dependence/ congruence – sources of the socio-human/ community cohesion, solidarity and humanity. Between the humane community and the individuals being established a humane/ cultural-ontological balance, an existential and functional optimum where are satisfied, ontologically, in a harmonious and non-confrontational way, both the personal and the collective necessities.

In the humanistic literature, the dominant conception is that, at least from the humanistic perspective, the great inclusive, cohesive and developed communities incorporate, in a sublime manner, both the features of the organizational/ institutional development and the features of the humane, cultural and moral development, representing, in this connection, great values and resources in the humanistic group therapy, in humanistic social work, humanistic management, etc. As well, regarding the humanistic representation of the person/ personality the dominant conception is that the great, developed, adaptive personalities incorporate, in a sublime manner, both the features of the strong personality, the psychological-personal development, and the features of the spiritual-humane personality, the spiritual-humane development - representing, in this connection, great values and resources in humanistic psychotherapy, education, social work, aesthetics, etc.

Regarding **the destination** of this paper, its design, content and bibliography are made in such a way that to be useful both to the academic community, to students and teachers, and also to the professional community, to psychotherapists, educators, managers, social workers, artists, etc.

Chapter 1

Sources and Models of the Humanistic Approach and Method in the Socio-Human Sciences and Practices

Content

The
Humanistic Approach
in
Psychology & Psychotherapy,
Sociology & Social Work,
Pedagogy & Education,
Management and Art:

Personal Development
and
Community Development

1.1. Introductory Aspects

In this book **humanism** (as rational thinking, through science, especially the socio-human sciences, and the human artistic creativity and imagination), **ontology** (as fundamental and constitutional domain of philosophy that has in its center of interest the category of *being, the existence in-itself*), the **philosophy of man** and the **social philosophy** (as theoretical-philosophical disciplines that study and interpret the man/ human and society in terms of ethical, metaphysical and ontological values and categories), **existentialism** and **phenomenology** (that promote the displacement of the interest from the abstract, metaphysical themes, toward the existential, phenomenological themes, toward the concrete, determined, existing, particular entities), the **human rights philosophy/ movement** (where all human beings are considered to be born free and equal in dignity and rights), the **secular humanism** and the **"Humanist Manifesto"** (that promote, from an atheistic position, the better rational understanding of ourselves, of our history, our intellectual and artistic achievements), **postmodernism** and **transmodernism** (where the social and human entities are considered to be very fluid, constantly in unpredictable changing) and the **oriental philosophies and practices** (where the aim of life is considered to be, principally, the inner fulfillment of the person) are considered as main *sources* and *models* of the humanistic approach and method in the socio-human sciences and practices, of humanistic psychology and psychotherapy, of humanistic sociology and humanistic social work, of humanistic pedagogy and education, of humanistic management, of humanistic aesthetics.

In literature is considered that phenomenology and existentialism had and have central role in the imposition and maintaining of the humanistic approach in the socio-human sciences and practices, especially with their concerns for the displacement of the interest from the abstract, metaphysical themes toward the existential, phenomenological themes, the interest for the particular human condition and nature, the concrete, unique person-society relationship, the emphasis on real, lived life, the interest in topics such as happiness and distress, the limit experiences, the existential crises and impasses, the willpower and ability to self-determination, freedom and responsibility, the limits of the personal freedom, the ontological congruence between person and environment, the concrete social existence, from the speculative philosophy towards the philosophy of the concrete, determined, existing, particular man, the primacy of the man as an individual, person, ego, and uniqueness in society, the interest for personal growing and autonomy, the power of reason, the self-knowledge, the self-actualization, the self-realization, etc.

1.2. Humanism

In its complex and large meaning humanism involves both the rational thinking, through science, especially the socio-human sciences, and the human artistic creativity and imagination.

As it is well known, in the social and human sciences, the term/ terms *humanism/ humanist/ humanistic/ etc.* has been consecrated through many meanings. In relation to the specific theme of the book we hold mainly two:

1) related to the *human* condition and nature, the idea of ancestral human unity and solidarity; the representation of the person as ontological part of a human community, mutual conditioned by the common/ unique human-genetic common background and specific inter-personal interactions - theoretical-axiological sources of the social/ human solidarity, humanity/ humanness, socio-human adaptation, and concern/ care for the other/ each other;

2) related to the intrinsic/ inner resources and capacities of the human as individual, as person, of affirmation, self-determination, personal accomplishment and development; the representation of the person as *me*, personality, with the attribute of will and freedom, creativity, responsibility and dignity - sources of the personal fulfillment, change and empowerment (of the individual and of the community) (A. Goodman, 1990).

The first meaning is, with predilection, exploited and stated by philosophy, religion, transpersonal psychology and anthropology, while the second by humanistic and positive psychology, pedagogy and psychotherapy. Both are exploited and stated by humanistic sociology, social work and management.

In agreement with the two established theoretical-axiological meanings the humanistic approach to the socio-human sciences and practices generates two relatively distinct perspectives of approach:

➢ *solidarist-humanistic*, and

➢ *existential/ positive-humanistic*.

Although, strictly analytically, seems somewhat opposite, in fact, the two forms, solidarist-humanistic and existential/ positive-humanistic, are "two faces of the same coin", two sides and dimensions of the same process, subsumed to a unitary theory and practice of the humanistic social and therapeutic sciences and practices, within the larger theoretical-methodological framework of the science of human as a whole.

Undoubtedly, the humanism, with its phenomenological and existentialist philosophical foundations, through all its artistic, social, philosophical, scientific, ideological, political, educational dimensions, manifestations and concerns, through the multitude of themes and meanings by which it was consecrated, as system or mode of thought and action predominating the human interests, the human values and dignity, as variety of ethical theories and practices that emphasize the human fulfillment through knowledge and social development, focusing on the person/ individual/ self, centering on the person's resources, the self-determination, human solidarity, humanity, human sensitivity, philanthropy, happiness, promoting the person's welfare, through the constitutional concern for researching the human being, his nature, essence, condition, through the interest for promoting of some great general human values and ideals in the evolution and development of society, through the interest for change and new, for truth, beautiful, good, represents one of the most important foundation and essential source of the humanistic approaches and methods in the social and therapeutic sciences and practices, of an authentic humanistic theory of the person and, personality, of the social relations and social groups, represented with all that created humanity in his history in domains as philosophy, art, science, anthropology, etc.

Referring to the role that it plays humanism in the fundamentation of the humanistic social theories and practices, especially of humanistic social work Malcolm Payne affirms:

„Humanism brings together rational thinking, through science, with artistic creativity and imagination; one is not more important than another. The aims of that constellation of human skills are the development of thought-out value systems, innovation, and critical evaluation of ideas and actions. Democracy, human rights, and personal liberty go alongside one another in helping us achieve personal fulfillment in our lives" (Payne, 2011, p. 5).

1.3. Ontology

Ontology is a fundamental and constitutional domain of philosophy, and has in its center of interest/ research/ knowledge the category of being, the existence in-itself. Most often, the domain is opposed to epistemology, which studies the knowledge in himself and the things mainly scientifically and categorically, opposed to the ontological approach.

From the ontological point of view the things, even the spiritual things, really exist, these have a nature, a beginning, a processual, determined, unique, unrepeatable existence (T. Hofweber, 2004), also a the end, while epistemology, in its purely position, claims that the things are rather representations and products of some intellectual or sensory-cognitive "processings", and, if the things and phenomena actually exist, are multiplications of some immutable structures, patterns, epistemologically subjected to certain intellectual and scientific processes of generalization, categorization, universalization.

Ontology is a conceptual-philosophical system yet underutilized in the modeling of the processes of formation, or in understanding and modeling the mode of functioning/ beingness of the person/ personality and the social group/ community. It could provide thus a framework for a lot of explanations and for solving many socio-human, educational and therapeutic problems. (D. Weissman, 2000)

We are talking about an ontological-phenomenological paradigm but also dynamic, with its central theme: the *theory of being*, (especially of the *human being*) and of existence, of the concrete fact, and namely of the concrete, unique human being, in process, in beingness and functioning.

Ontology favors the interest for the real, unique, concrete person and social community, with their particular, specific, unique feelings, emotions and socio-human contexts and relationships, imposing an idiographic-empirical/ emergentical paradigm, whereas epistemology favors the representation of the person or the socio-human community, in general the socio-human phenomenon, through universalization, globalization, through scientific categories such as structure, system, function, institution, social control, recurrence, nomological approach.

Therefore, regarding the representation of the person, personality and socio-human community, their formation, the ontological theory/ paradigm highlights, mostly, the following aspects:

- the person, the personality, the community, the organization, etc. are unique, emergent products of the particular, contextual ontogenesis, and not simple "embodiments" of some universal, transpersonal patterns, structures, models;

- as existence the persons and groups lives, coexists, firstly, among/ through complex, unpredictable humans, persons, living beings, with soul, with specific and unique needs, dramas, attachments, and personality, and only indirectly in social structures, institutions, systems.

Ontology has consecrated/ established/ proposed, among others, the paradigmatic ontological triad: *being-existent-existence (being in itself - being for itself - being outside-itself)*.

In ontological perspective **the being** (being in itself) of an entity represents the essence, the original content, the invariable, the ontological-metaphysical foundation of the entities, of the existent and of the existence, **the existent/ existing** (being for itself) represents the organization, the concrete form, unique, part of a context, the exposed side of the being, acquiring the characteristics of form of the concrete environment where it exists, while **the existence**, or **the beingness** (being outside-itself), represents the processual, contingental, situational-contextual side, exposed time, dynamic, experiential, the feeling and the thinking. (Maritain, 1956; Hegel, 1977).

In agreement with the metaphysical-ontological paradigm outlined above, regarding the representation of the person we will consider that *the ontological-psychological sphere* (the self, the ego) represents *the being* of the person, *the psychological-personal sphere* (the conscience, personality, the skills) represents *the existent/ existing*, while *the experiential-behavioral sphere* (the functioning, the beingness, the current life/ activity/ experience of the person, its jouissance, feelings, concrete processual thinking) represents *the existence*.

The paradigm can be applied similarly also to the socio-human community/ organization.

1.4. The Philosophy of Man and the Social Philosophy

An important theoretical-philosophical fundamentation and source of the humanistic approaches and methods in the socio-human sciences and practice, is the (Humanistic) **Philosophy of Man/ Human.**

Therefore, the philosophy of man represents, important theoretical and methodological foundation and source for a *humanistic* theory and representation of the concrete man/ human, of the person (Reichmann, 1985), of a person with personality, ego and soul, of a person who lives and suffers and not of a person who is a simple element into a social system/ mechanism.

Social Philosophy is, as theoretical-philosophical discipline, the study and interpretation of society and social institutions in terms of ethical, metaphysical and ontological values and categories rather than in empirical or scientific terms, being a branch of philosophy that explores, therefore ethically, metaphysically and ontologically, issues of socio-human community/ group/ organization, social behavior, social institutions, addressing aspects like how the persons, as social beings, behave and empathize mutually in groups, communities, society environments, etc. (L. Thomas, 2007).

1.5. Existentialism and Phenomenology

Phenomenology and existentialism was released, promoted and developed by thinkers such as Kierkegaard, Husserl, Heidegger, Sartre, de Beauvoir, Merleau-Ponty, Nietzsche etc., with their concerns for:

- The human condition and nature;
- The person-society relationships;
- Emphasis on real, lived life;
- Interest in topics such as happiness and distress;
- The limit experiences;
- The existential crises and impasses;
- The willpower and ability to self-determination;
- Freedom and responsibility;
- The limits of the personal freedom;

- The ontological congruence between person and environment;

- The concrete social existence;

- The displacement of the interest from the abstract, metaphysical themes, towards the existential, phenomenological themes;

- From the speculative philosophy towards the philosophy of the concrete, determined, existing, particular man;

- The primacy of the man as an individual, person, ego, and uniqueness in society;

- The limits of the human being, the human being's fragility;

- Interest for personal growing and autonomy;

- The power of reason, the self-knowledge, the self-realization, the self-actualization, etc. (Heidegger, 1962; E. Husserl, D. Moran, 2012)

1.6. The Human Rights Philosophy/ Movement

Many of the ideas and values stipulated above can be found in *The Universal Declaration of Human Rights*, which constitute, too, important sources and supports for the humanistic approach and method in psychology and psychotherapy, sociology and social work, pedagogy and education, management and art, also for a humanistic approach on personal development and community development.

Below we select and enumerate the most relevant stipulations in connection with the most important categories and aspects of the the humanistic approach and method in these important socio-human sciences and practices.

❖ *All human beings are born free and equal in dignity and rights. They are endowed with reason and conscience and should act towards one another in a spirit of brotherhood.*

❖ *Everyone has the right to life, liberty and security of person.*

❖ *Everyone has the right to a standard of living adequate for the health and well-being of himself and of his family, including food, clothing, housing and medical care and necessary social services, and the right to security in the event of unemployment, sickness, disability, widowhood, old age or other lack of livelihood in circumstances beyond his control.*

❖ *Everyone has duties to the community in which alone the free and full development of his personality is possible.*

❖ *In the exercise of his rights and freedoms, everyone shall be subject only to such limitations as are determined by law solely for the purpose of securing due recognition and respect for the rights and freedoms of others and of meeting the just requirements of morality, public order and the general welfare in a democratic society (www.un.org/en/ documents/udhr/).*

1.7. The Secular Humanism. The "Humanist Manifesto"

Essentially and constitutionally, the secular humanism is described through its opposition to religion and the way of life and thinking that it promotes, sustaining the scientific methods rather than faith and mysticism in seeking solutions to the human problems, to the most important human aspects of the life.

The secular humanism promotes the better rational understanding of ourselves, of our history, our intellectual and artistic achievements, promotes the thesis that with reason, science and technique we can create an open marketplace of goods, ideas, and tolerance, a world for all people.

Therefore, in the secular humanism's perspective the progress can be made by building a better world for all the people, without discrimination of sex, nationality, race or ethnicity, sexual orientation, etc.

In science and philosophy the secular humanism promotes the principle, the philosophy called *naturalism*, in which the physical laws of the universe are not superseded by non-material or supernatural entities such as demons, gods, or other "spiritual" beings outside the realm of the natural universe (P. Kurtz, 2006).

These ideas, principles and theses are represented also in the well known *"Humanist Manifesto"* (I, II, and III). Principally, the three *Manifestos* outline the aspects that:

- the humans and the communities are guided firstly by reason;

- the humans are an integral part of nature, the result of unguided evolutionary change;

- the ethical values are derived from human need and interest as tested by experience;

- the life's fulfillment emerges from the individual participation in the service of humane ideals;

- the humans are social by nature and find meaning in relationships;

- working to benefit society maximizes individual happiness. (http://americanhumanist.org/humanism/humanist_manifesto_iii).

1.8. Postmodernism and Transmodernism

Undoubtedly, the postmodern and the transmodern philosophical, sociological and cultural thinking have a crucial role in the axiological-theoretical and methodological support and fundamentation of the humanistic approach and method in the socio-human sciences and practices (T. Schick, 1999).

In the contemporary socio-human thought and practices the **postmodernism** is identifiable, inter alia, by the following ideas and values (we strake only those that are relevant to the theme of the book):

- The society, the community, the social group etc. are very complex and unpredictable entities, without clear, accurate goals and objectives;

- The human society is a fragmented existence, discontinuous and uneven;

- The social dynamics is very fluid, the social entity is constantly in changing, the social entity cannot be epistemologically modeled (Beck, 1992);

- It prevails the indeterminacy and the irrational;

- The relations between institutions and people are ambivalent and uncertain;

- Prevails the hedonism and the moral/ cultural relativism;

- The primary interest of the individual before the interests of the society etc.

The **transmodern** philosophical, sociological and cultural thought, comes, inter alia, with philosophical and paradigmatic solutions which, without contempt the postmodern paradigms calls for a reassessment, in the cyber and globalization age, of the great universal values that have marked the history of the world, such as family, love, solidarity, altruism, cooperation etc. (Schick, 1999).

1.9. The Oriental Philosophies and Practices

The oriental philosophies and practices, especially those regarding the perspective on the life and the interpersonal relationships have penetrated in the western social and therapeutic sciences and practices especially in the second half of the twentieth century, influencing/ determining, in important measure, especially the (humanistic) psychotherapeutic and medical ideas and practices.

If the western traditional/ classical approaches and methods have an external and technical orientation, the oriental approaches and methods have mostly an internal heuristic orientation, largely concerning religious and philosophical issues, using in great measure holistic intuitive methods.

If in the western traditional/ classical approaches and methods the reference point is the average person, the normal being the average, in the oriental axiology, approaches and methods the normal is the ideal, the perfection.

In this sense, the cultivation/ empowerment of the quality of the subjective experience is the main concern, the aim of life being considered to be, principally, the self-realization, the self-actualization, the self-accomplishment, the inner fulfillment of the person (J.M. Koller, 1985).

Therefore, with the development of the humanistic approach especially in psychology, psychotherapy and counseling great part of the oriental writings, philosophies, techniques and practices has become very relevant, useful and was adopted and adapted in theory and practice.

Chapter 2

The Specifics of the Humanistic Approach and Method in the Socio-Human Sciences and Practices

Content

The
Humanistic Approach
in
Psychology & Psychotherapy,
Sociology & Social Work,
Pedagogy & Education,
Management and Art:

Personal Development
and
Community Development

2.1. Introductory Aspects

Essentially, the humanistic approach and method in the socio-human sciences and practices proposes, from the existential-positive position the representation of the person and personality through traits like high level of personal development, high capacity to self-determination, high resilience, high capacity to control the emotions, etc., and the socio-human micro-community through features such as strong organizational culture, high functionality, high cohesion, unity, solidity, adaptability, resilience, high autonomy, resistance to crisis and challenges, good management, etc., while from the ontological/spiritual (cultural) position it is highlighted especially the inner-ontological psychological-spiritual and psychological-humane content/ valence/ dimension of the personality, of the spiritual and humane self, and the inter-personal relationships of attachment, love, respect, the dominance of the practices and customs of mutual helps in community.

In the humanistic practices and researches the *analytic-inductive methods* are the principal scientific-methodological tools. This method may combines the rigor with the complexity, the general with the particular, leading to more relevant and useful results for the specific characteristics of the social and human phenomena and processes, taking both from the rigor of the quantitative techniques but also from the deepness, flexibility and comprehensivity of the qualitative techniques.

The specifics of the qualitative, interpretative and comprehensive methods in the socio-human sciences and practices is mainly that it focuses largely on capturing the *phenomena* more than the essences, the universal laws; the object of evaluation, observation and investigation being most often the event, the socio-human context, the sentiment, the concrete attitudes, feelings and reactions of people being in determined social and human relationships and processes.

The advantage is that through this approach is obtained the access to social and human aspects which would escape to an eminently nomological, scientific-technical approach, more focused on capturing the structural, universal and repeatable evidences.

2.2. The Humanistic Approach in the Socio-Human Sciences and Practices - **Core Specific Concepts and Ideas**

Among the most significant concepts, ideas and terms of the humanistic approach and method in psychology and psychotherapy, sociology and social work, pedagogy and education, management, and art are *personality, social relations, personal development* and *community development*.

So, a crucial concept of the humanistic approach and method in the socio-human sciences and practices, especially in psychology and psychotherapy, pedagogy and education is **Personality**.

Generally, the term is used most often to refer to the ensemble of constant psychological and behavioral characteristics of an individual, highlighting, with preference, the aspects of unity of the behavior in different situations, and dominance/ consistency of certain features, especially from the temperament and character spheres (Allport, 1961; Maslow, 2011).

From the humanistic perspective it is highlighted the importance of self/ ego as core/ central instances in the internal structure and functioning/ economy of personality (Friedman & Schustack, 2010; McAdams, 2009).

If the structural-functionalist, or cognitive-behavioral approaches emphasize either the role of the body structure or the structural neuro-cognitive factors, either that of the structural societal, cultural, educational factors, representing mostly in a cybernetical way the human personality (Zheng, 2012), either as a reflection of the structure and physiology of the body or brain, or as a automatic product of the socio-cultural environment wherein was formed the personality, through learning, imitation and internalization of the dominant/ characteristic social roles and behaviors (Burkitt, 1991), the humanistic approach highlights especially the inner-ontological psychological-spiritual and psychological-humane content/ valence/ dimension of the personality, of the spiritual self, of the soul, their aesthetic, playful, moral or religious resources, focusing, especially, on personal development and social adaptation by using the psycho-volitional and cognitive-adaptive resources of the ego-personality and conscience.

In this sense, the complex humanistic approach to personality highlights and promotes personality traits and qualities such as optimism, energy, free will, liberty, autonomy, self-determination, self-realization, hope, positive thinking, activity, consciousness, responsibility, empathy, humanity, altruism, etc.

The concept **Human Relations**, very important in humanistic social work and management, is as complex as vague, including a very large area of issues and topics, from the simple inter-personal relations to aspects and themes such as attachment, empathy, or complex phenomena of group or society like social solidarity and humanity. The optimal framework of their manifestations is the *micro-community* (Mayo, 1933).

In the *humanistic* approach the term human relations is used for ideas and situations such as the social and interpersonal relationships between *human* beings, the study of group behavior in order to improve the interpersonal relationships etc., while the term *microcommunity* is represented mostly as a small socio-human group of persons closely related by subjective interests, needs, etc. In the most socio-human microcommunities people sharing similar characteristics, and collectively have a sense of human/humane unity/solidarity (Znaniecki, 1969, 94). It exhibits a high degree of socio-human cohesion and is more than a simple collection or aggregate of individuals.

In the scientific literature, the concept of **Personal Development** is associated or identified with a number of other concepts such as psychic development, growth, adaptation, social development etc.

It is a crucial category of the humanist-positive current from the social and human sciences and practices, and, regarding the professional from the humanistic social and therapeutic practices, implies, highlights, the followings:

- High degree of awareness, self-knowledge, self-esteem (Maslaw);

- Maximizing and capitalizing of the internal potential of development, self-actualization, optimization, personal and social efficiency (Rogers);

- Psychological-emotionally well-being, satisfaction, happiness, hedonism (Seligman);

- Socio-emotional development, control of emotions, emotional intelligence (Erikson);

- Realism and balance;

- Powerful will, resistance to failure and frustrations;

- Hope, projectivity, orientation towards the future;

- Positive attitude, optimism, active thinking;

- Moral development;

- Aesthetic sensitivity;

- Maximal capitalization of the skills and talents;

- Professional development;

- Personal and social autonomy;

- Interpersonal development;

- Mature personality, adaptability;

- Overcoming the crisis, reducing the existential anxieties (Frankl).

The term **Community Development** is associated or identified with a number of other concepts such as:

- social development;

- socio-human growth;

- integration and adaptation;

- organizational development;

- strong community;

- developed community;

- community empowerment;

- democratic leadership;

- social and community autonomy;

- interpersonal development;

- group development;

- mature community;

- strong capacity to overcoming the crisis;

- strong capacity to reducing the conflicts. (M. Ledwith, 2005).

Community development, increasing the quality of the socio-human relationships, the transformation of the *social* relationships and communities in *humane* relationships and communities are, in our opinion, very important resources of the humanistic social practices, especially in social work and management (Stefaroi, 2012, p. 166).

2.3. The Humanistic-Existential Orientation

The humanistic-existential paradigm of the person and personality, of the human relations and human microcommunity, originated in existential psychology and sociology, focuses specifically on personal/ personality and community development and personal/ social adjustment through the use of the psychological/ organizational and adaptive resources, highlighting, therefore, the existential and cohesive dimension in the psycho-social behavior, relationships and microcommunity as entity, unity in the macrosocial/societal context.

This humanistic paradigm highlights community traits and characteristic such as unity, cohesion, resistance to crises and challenges, strong community and strong human relationships, community development etc. (Vanier, 1989, 304) – crucial values and resources in humanistic social work and management practice, and psychological-personal features as high self-control, socio-emotional development, realism and balance, powerful will, resistance to failure and frustrations, positive attitude, optimism, active thinking, professional development, interpersonal development, mature personality, adaptability, high capacity to overcoming the crisis and conflicts, etc.

As value-objective of practice the strong/ developed personality and microcommunity applied to the field of humanistic psychotherapy and education, to humanistic social work, management and art helps to a better understanding of the relationship between the client and the living environment, representing it by traits like functionality, integration, autonomy etc.

In psychotherapy the humanistic-existential paradigm of the client, originated in the existential and positive (phenomenological) philosophy, determines the focalization of intervention on personal development and social adjustment through the use of the psycho-volitional and adaptive resources, highlighting, therefore, its existential and adaptive dimension, the freedom, responsibility and the will of the client to overcome the situation of difficulty (Allport, 1961, 560; Snyder & Lopez, 2006).

To this end, one of the most important aim of the therapy is to contribute to the development of psychological-personal and behavioral traits and qualities such as activism, self-determination, freedom-accountability, optimism, energy, free will, self-realization, hope, active consciousness, personal development, social adaptability, assertiveness, resilience, happiness etc. (Seligman and Csikszentmihalyi, 2000; Schellhamme, 2012; Seligman, 2002, 99).

2.4. The Humanistic-Spiritual/ Cultural Orientation

In **sociology, social work** and **management** this approach highlights especially the ontological-humane-cultural content of the human relation or microcommunity, giving, as is natural, to the ontological-humane and cultural sphere the primary etiological, structural and existential role.

The humanistic-ontological approach of the human relations and microcommunity brings in the theory, methodology and practice of humanistic social work and management aspects, ideas and solutions as:

- the socio-emotional processes and phenomena in relationships and groups;

- the relations of attachment between persons;

- how people actually live, love, suffer;

- the inter-empathetical processes and phenomena (Gerdes & Segal, 2011, 146).

As value-objective of practice the human relations and the microcommunity applied to the field of humanistic social work and management helps to a better and profound understanding of the relationships between the client/ employee and the living/ organizational environment, representing them, in the existential/ positive version, by traits such as harmony, unity, congruence, attachment.

In **humanistic psychology/ psychotherapy** and **humanistic pedagogy/ education** this orientation highlights especially the ontological-psychological, human-spiritual and transpersonal dimension/content of personality (Cortright, 1997, 123).

According to Rogers (1980), the key and structural concept of the humanistic-ontological theory of personality is the *self*. Maslow (2011), indicates an important gap in the academic/ scientific psychology theory and method, namely the relatively lack in the structure and composition of the personality, of its ontological-spiritual content, of its *being,* humanity.

In this context he envisaged that the future of the psychology, implicitly of the psychotherapy, also of other areas of the social practices (education, social work, management, etc.) will depend, to a large extent, of the concerns and performances of redefining the personality theory/model/paradigm, where to the ontological-spiritual and human dimension/ sphere will need to be given much more attention.

2.5. Complex and Emergent Systems Theories

Essentially, these kind of theories highlight the aspects that the systems (especially the living and spiritual systems) consist of many interrelated and interdependent components or parts, linked through many (dense) and often chaotic interconnections (J.C. Smuts, 1973).

The emergent and complex systems cannot be described by simple rules, laws, and their characteristics are not reducible to one level of description. They exhibit properties that emerge from the interaction of their parts and which cannot be predicted from the properties of the parts (Ludwig von Bertalanffy, 1968).

In these theories (which include, among others, the chaos theory and the holistic theory) the formation of the person/ personality, of the human being (in our humanistic-ontological theory) involve characteristics, properties, processes, principles such as onto-formatization, persomization and promergence, emergence and imergence, transmergence and telegence, conmergence and sinmergence, and ontological stages of evolution, development, establishment of the personal ontological-psychological formations, of the person as a whole, such as of contact, of acquisition/ accumulation, of structuration/ centralization, of constitution/ holistization, of establishing/ networking, of ontification/ fulfillment.

In the light of these theories the processes take place, largely, without limitations and physical barriers of "space", time and organization, transcending the structures, the organizations, and the entities already constituted, attracting and involving them in the processes of forming, constituting and establishing of the new formations, without altering them (J. Gleick, 1987).

In humanistic personology, the ontological-humanistic perspective on the process of formation of the person/ personality, the degree of freedom/ action is very large, the number of combinations and the facilities of structuration and formatization being almost unlimited; one of the most important explanation is given by the fact that in the emergent and complex systems the processes have the extraordinary quality to permit the transcendence and the multiplication to infinit of the informational/ spiritual entities, taking place without time limitations and barriers, by the fact/ explanation that the processes have the tendency to organize and concentrate them "thematically" in formations, persoms, structures, spheres etc., reflecting the inherence, the objective necessity of some functions, beyond any limitations of "logistic" or temporal order, the entities coexist, simultaneously, in the same personal "space", the functioning and beingness of some distinct entities, structures, relationships, processes on/ through the same material, biological, informational, spiritual support, framework.

The humane and spiritual experiences and the promergent processes are involved in complex, emergent, dynamic mechanisms and entities, every formation, sphere, personality, the person as a whole being so a product of the ontogenetical incorporation, union, synthesis, of the conmergent, emergent, transmergent unitary organization of the sub-entities/ formations, structures, energies, mechanisms, of the processes of organization in new structures, formative entities, formations, spheres, usually upper structurally and axiologically.

Too, in humanistic sociology, the ontological-humanistic perspective on the process of formation of the socio-human community, the degree of freedom/ action is very large, the number of combinations and the facilities of social structuration and formatization being almost unlimited.

In the emergent and complex systems the processes have the extraordinary quality to organize and concentrate them "thematically" in social formations, structures, institutions etc., reflecting the inherence, the objective necessity of some functions, beyond any limitations of "logistic" or temporal order, the entities coexist, simultaneously, in the same social and cultural "space" (J. Gleick, 1987).

The socio-human, cultural and institutional experiences are involved in complex, emergent, dynamic mechanisms and entities, every social formation and structure, the community as a whole is a product of the ontogenetical incorporation, union, synthesis, of the conmergent, emergent, transmergent unitary organization of the sub-entities/ formations, structures, energies, mechanisms, of the processes of organization in new socio-human structures, entities, institutions, usually, too, upper structurally and culturally.

2.6. Methodology

Florian Znaniecki (1934), the founder of humanistic sociology, proposes the *analytic-inductive method* as principal scientific-methodological tool in the socio-human sciences and practices, of evaluation and intervention, of research of the socio-human processes and phenomena.

This method may combines the rigor with the complexity, the general with the particular, leading to more relevant and useful results for the specific characteristics of the social and human phenomena and processes, taking both from the rigor of the quantitative techniques but also from the deepness, flexibility and comprehensivity of the qualitative techniques.

In evaluation and research the main goal being that, through analysis, analogies, comparisons, exclusions, similarities, differences, observations of great extension and profoundness, to extract, with great caution, several relevant regularities, to serve eventually to the formulation of some minimal empirical statistical conclusions, laws, evaluative predictions or intervention projects.

The specifics of the qualitative, interpretative and comprehensive methods in the socio-human sciences and practices is mainly that it focuses largely on capturing the *phenomena* more than the essences, universal laws; the object of evaluation, observation and investigation being most often the event, the socio-human context, the sentiment, the concrete attitudes, feelings and reactions of people being in determined social and human relationships and processes.

The advantage is that through this methodology is obtained the access to social and human aspects which would escape to an eminently positive, nomological, scientific-technical approach, more focused on capturing the structural, universal and repeatable evidences, by modelations of mathematical type (Denzin & Lincoln, 2005).

2.7. The Specifics of Research

Of great importance in the humanistic social sciences is the aspect referring to the specifics of research and the specifics of the professional/services activities of evaluation and intervention based on its results.

Even if at first glance the humanistic approach in the social sciences seems somewhat incompatible with the scientific research in fact their finds can represent very useful knowledge and means of the activity of evaluation, design and of the day-to-day practice in working with the clients.

Regarding the issue of importance, relevance and role of some factors like personality and human relations, as basic values and resources of the practice, are very welcome and used the results of some scientific and/or clinical studies and investigations related to:

- the relation between personality (the personality type) and the social resilience/ adaptation/integration of the persons (clients) (Campbell-Sills, Cohan & Stein, 2006; Lazarus, 1961; Connor-Smith & Flachsbart, 2007);

- the relation between personality and the professional adaptation/ efficiency/ resilience in the assistential, therapeutic, social, humanitarian activities (of the professionals) (Connor-Smith & Flachsbart, 2007; Barrick & Mount, 1991);

- the relation between different types of internal social/human relationships and the resilience, cohesion and functionality of community (family, care institution, professional organization etc.) (Reis, Collins & Berscheid, 2000);

- the relation between the type and the human quality of the community and the adaptation, effectiveness and happiness of its members (Molinari, 1998; Magee, James & Scerri, 2012).

As specific, in the humanistic social and therapeutic sciences and practices, including regarding the role of personality and human relations as values and resources of practice, as in any paradigm, practice or science of humanistic type, the research is approached somewhat differently than in the social practices, paradigms and sciences of non-humanistic, positive orientation, or in the natural sciences.

Because of the complexity of the socio-human relationships and phenomena, the personality, the human experience cannot be easily and rigorously investigated and captured by figures, numbers the research is so forced to appeal often to methods of *qualitative, narrative, analytical, subjective, interpretative* or *phenomenological* type.

2.8. The Specifics of Evidence-Based Practices

In the humanistic social and therapeutic practices the results of researches, whether they are products of some studies or investigations of quantitative, strictly scientific type, or of some studies or investigations of qualitative, comprehensive, phenomenological or clinical type, are used especially in what was consecrated as *the practices based on research*, or *on evidences*.

Despite appearances, the professionals and services use the scientific methodology, the researches' findings and the evidence-based practice.

It is uses the evidence-based practices and methods to understand and address, scientifically and experimentally, especially aspects such as the client's contextual human relationships and behavior, the client's human growth/ development in deferent type of communities, the interpretation and modelation the clients' situations of difficulty, etc. ((Payne, 2011, 46; Roberts & Yeager, 2006, 196).

The construction of the *evaluative/ diagnostic table* starts, yet, with what is identified as *existing, real, concrete* and *sensitive*. (Payne, 2011, 76). Further, the practitioner's work is based on the (scientific or clinical) researches and studies' conclusions upon the type of case it works.

This having the task to realize "modelations" of the identified difficult situations in report to the researches' findings without abdicating but from the fundamental values and principles of the humanistic methodology related to the immense complexity of the human being, of the socio-human phenomenon, of the client's personality, of the specific, concrete human relationships where it lives (O'Hare, 2005, 153; Rubin and Babbi, 2012, 233).

Finally, in the *specific and concrete activity of intervention and change* the practices based on researches and evidences propose, aim, the focalization on the *concrete, complex* and *phenomenological socio-human reality* of the client (person or group) but *by means of the scientific and clinical knowledge,* through embedding in activity *the conclusions of the relevant and useful researches,* of the previous scientific and clinical studies and experiences, *relevant* and *effective* for the respective client system, case, problem, situation of difficulty, or of learning in the case of humanistic education/ pedagogy.

Chapter 3

The Humanistic Approach and Method
in Psychology and Psychotherapy

Content

The
Humanistic Approach
in
Psychology & Psychotherapy,
Sociology & Social Work,
Pedagogy & Education,
Management and Art:

*Personal Development
and
Community Development*

3.1. Introductory Aspects

Psychology and psychotherapy has experienced in the second half of the twentieth century radical changes, in a large extent determined by the offensive of so-called *humanistic theory and method* in all the areas of the social sciences and practices.

With old origins even in antiquity, passing through Renaissance, and then reinvigorated by phenomenology and existentialism, the humanistic thinking and method have manifested powerfully initially in psychology as theory, instituting the humanistic psychology and, consequently, in psychotherapy, as the third way alongside psychoanalysis and behaviorism, both in theory and practice.

Therefore, how psychotherapy are "alimented", theoretically-methodologically, largely, from psychology, as theory and science, inevitably, directly or indirectly, their humanistic values, theories and methodology have made the presence increasingly in practice, redimensioning and reforming them, gradually and subtly, almost entirely, the humanistic theory and methodology succeeded, so gradually, to make place in the psychotherapy's literature and practice through values, objectives and terms such as *self-actualization, empowerment, accountability, human and personal development, happiness, self-determination, client-centered intervention* etc., also to determine even a shift of emphasis to values and goals such as *client's empowerment, human rehabilitation/ development, happiness, personal development of the person/ client,* etc.

What particularizes the humanistic methodology, in addition to the system of specific theory and method, is the human/ humane/ spiritual and humanistic-positive system of values and resources, which must, ultimately, to generate *the change*, the empowerment, the human rehabilitation and the reintegration, promoting as resources and values, on the one hand the *human personality*, the person, the individuality, the self/ego, the soul, the character, the skills, the will and the conduct, of the client as well of the professional, and, on the other hand, especially in humanistic group therapy, the *human, inter-human, inter-personal relationships*, the human relations lesser understood as mere social relations and mostly as *humane* relationships, generators of empowerment, human-psychological, personal development and happiness - resources for whose use the therapists appeal to ways of empowerment such as the empathy, the inter-empathy, the transfer, the psycho-social influence, etc.

Personality, as core category, values and resource is addressed in this chapter of the book by the two cardinal guidelines of the humanistic theory, respectively *existential-positive* and *ontological-spiritual/ humane*, speaking, therefore, in humanistic-ontological perspective of *spiritual/ humane personality*, and, in existential-positive perspective of *strong* and *developed personality*. The resilience and the change being obtained by the mobilization, development and control of these resources in the therapeutic process.

Too, a core concept in humanistic psychology, as personality trait, as well of the humanistic psychotherapy as objective but also as resource is *Personal Development*, that in this chapter is approached in close relation to the concept of *Strong Personality*, implying features as personal and social efficiency, socio-emotional development, high control of emotions, emotional intelligence, realism and balance, powerful will, resistance to failure and frustrations, hope, orientation to future. positive attitude, optimism, active thinking, high degree of awareness, self-knowledge, self-esteem, professional development, personal and social autonomy, interpersonal development, mature personality, adaptability.

To achieve these objectives the humanistic psychotherapy operates mainly with therapeutic methods or modalities like person-centered psychotherapy/ counseling, existential psychotherapy/ counseling, gestalt therapy and group psychotherapy, transpersonal and spiritual psychotherapy, positive psychotherapy, and experiential psychotherapy.

One of the most important ways of intervention in humanistic psychotherapy is the emancipation, empowerment and development of the client through its (re-) spiritualization and humanization, through spiritual and human/ humane empowerment and development. Even if is a very complex and difficult endeavor, the humanization, spiritualization and humane-spiritual/cultural integration/ development of the person/ client is described by the therapists, for some categories of clients, as miraculous solutions for many kinds of problems, sufferings, deviances, etc.

Therefore, the epistemological foundation of the evaluation in humanistic psychotherapy is the representation of the client as *complex personality*. In humanistic therapy the practitioner, through *his* complex personality, contributes crucially to the achievement of the humanistic established objectives, mostly those relating to the personal and spiritual development of the client, the empowerment and autonomization, the social, socio-humane integration and adaptation in the community where the it lives.

Through his personality, behavior, creativity and empathy the humanistic therapist works at the construction of a new (psychological-personal) *modus vivendi*, of some new (socio-human) behaviors, even of a new personality, with *humanistic* (existential and spiritual) tools and methods.

To this end, the level of development of the spiritual-empathetic traits of the professional, in any philosophy or theoretical orientation, form, doctrine of therapy, represents essential predictors of effectiveness and fulfillment of the objectives, the more in humanistic therapy, where this quality/ resource of the professional exceeds the original psychosocial meaning, instituting so as a core value-resource of the efficiency in practice.

3.2. Humanistic Psychology – *the Third Force*

Humanistic psychology, often called "the third force" in psychology after psychoanalysis and behaviorism (Bugental, 1964; Maslow, 1968), promotes mainly the representation of the person as *ego* and *personality*, the power of the consciousness and of the will, the freedom, responsibility and self-determination, the development of the person in accordance with its characteristics and choices.

The humanistic method and approach to psychology reject the assumptions of the behaviorist perspective which is characterized as social/ external-deterministic, focused on stimulus-response behavior, also rejecte the psychodynamic approach because it is biological-deterministic, with unconscious irrational and instinctive forces that are considered to be determinant for the person's thought and behavior (Bugental, 1964).

Behaviorism and psychoanalysis are regarded therefore as dehumanized approaches and methods by the promoters of humanistic psychology, neglecting the importance of the ego, conscience and personality in the person's thinking and behavior.

Instead, from the humanistic psychology's position, every healthy individual has, inherently, an Ego and a Personality, and through these the capacity of self-determination, the capacity to achieve its potential in human, social and spiritual terms; all depending to its internal activism and of the willingness for change or self-fulfillment (Plotnik and Kouyoumdjian, 2007).

These are also some of the main resources of the humanistic psychology and its applications in psychotherapy, which brings in the forefront of clinical knowledge and therapeutic action concepts and ideas such as person-centered approach, self-determination, self-actualization, the power/ force of the ego, personality, and consciousness, strength-based interventions, spirituality, empowerment, personal development, personal accomplishment, holistic assessment and intervention, optimism, creativity, happiness, the individual/ client uniqueness, focus on the particular aspects of the human existence, tolerance, love, etc. (Maslow, 1968; Bugental, 1964; Rogers, 1959).

The theories of development and empowerment, empathy theory and happiness theory support, theoretically, in great measure, the humanistic psychology and psychotherapy.

The Theories of Personality/ Personal Development represent in humanistic psychology/ psychotherapy theoretical models and supports for approaching of the person/ client as human being under development, with the personality and conscience as core resources for growing, with ego, will, character, sensibility and empathy, and not as a simple reply of the human race, or a mere individual being in a simple social, organizational interaction.

In general, in humanistic psychology/ psychotherapy, the humanistic representation of the personality, approached as resource of development and empowerment, is imposed, according to our observations, by two main theories/ orientations/ approaches. One is the *positive/ existential-psychological* theory, another is the *ontological-spiritual* theory.

According to Rogers, Maslaw, Allport and other representatives of humanistic psychology and psychotherapy the need to achieving personal fulfillment is a crucial way for social and human rehabilitation of the client. Personal development is, so, one of the key tool of psychological rehabilitation and social adaptation of the person/ client.

Empathy theory is a formative instrument used by the professionals in achieving the specific objectives, mainly in the psychological-human rehabilitation and social empowerment of the client. The professional-client proactive psychological-empathetic relationship is in fact a framework for transfer, a subtle lane that the professional uses, intentionally and professionally, for solve the client's problem (Gerdes, Segal, 2011).

Crucial is the goal of psychological-personal rehabilitation and social/ compathetic integration of the client through its humanization, through spiritual development, through the development of empathetic spheres of his personality and behavior.

About empathy as psychosocial concept and phenomenon have dealt great thinkers like Lipps (to feel himself in something), Allport (understanding and feeling each other), Titchener (ability to think and feel what another person thinks and feels), Rogers (the fourth stage in the emotional-personal development; ability to really sit in the other's place, of seeing the world as he sees it), Batson (disposition/ motivation oriented to the other).

Hoffman (2000) interprets the empathic disposition of the person as effect of cognitive-affective action of the other, resulting so an emotional response closer to the other's interests than the self.

Most of the authors give the following meanings to the concept of empathy: sympathetic projection of the self, emotional fusion, sympathetic intuition, affective union, knowledge by interweaving, introjection, tranzitivism, intropathy, sympathy, transposition into the current other's state, identification with another, transfer, sympathetic projection.

Empathy is a form of knowledge of the environment, so is a cognitive process, is a form of feeling and emotional experience to the other, therefore, an emotional process, is an interpersonal process, so is a social process and, not least, a spiritual process/ phenomenon, through the human capacity to resonate to culture, science, philosophy, religion etc. All these phenomena and processes contribute to the establishment of what might be called the human sensitivity.

The practitioner uses the proactive, formative, educational and inductive valences of the empathy for the reconstruction, human-psychologically and social-compathetically, the personality, as step in the personal development and social/ human rehabilitation of the client.

The Happiness Theory as theory of psycho-social and philosophical-eudaimonical type, is based on the assumption that the efficiency and the personal/ professional/ social adaptation of the person in socio-human context is closely related to the degree of happiness, satisfaction and complacency (M.E. Seligman, 2002).

To this end, the psychological-spiritual well-being is a factor of energy and self-development/ autonomy, so reducing the degree of social vulnerability and the likelihood to becoming a client.

The relevance and usefulness of the happiness theory in humanistic psychotherapy is sustained by the fact that it is based on the following ideas, facts, principles:

- Every person, regardless of age, sex, nationality, race, social status, profession is entitled to a dignified life, to happiness, to personal fulfillment;

- The essential indicator of the human life quality is the internal satisfaction, subjective felt, the happiness and complacency of the person;

- The authentic happiness is a source of personal development, social/ professional efficiency and factor for the acquisition of the autonomous social reintegration capacity;

- The person is not only a simple consumer of services, of material goods, it is also a cultural, spiritual, aesthetic, playful being – this has, therefore, emotional, cultural, spiritual, aesthetic, playful needs too, that, for a full rehabilitation, fulfillment and happiness, must be unconditionally satisfied (M.E. Seligman, P. Csikszentmihalzi, 2000).

3.3. The *Five Core Principles* of Humanistic Psychology

An important moment in the history of humanistic psychology and its imposition as an autonomous discipline is the postulation of what was consecrated as *the five core principles* of humanistic psychology, in the "Journal of Humanistic Psychology" by James Bugental, in 1964, respectively:

- *Human beings, as human, supersede the sum of their parts. They cannot be reduced to components.*

- *Human beings have their existence in a uniquely human context, as well as in a cosmic ecology.*

- *Human beings are aware and are aware of being aware - i.e., they are conscious. Human consciousness always includes an awareness of oneself in the context of other people.*

- *Human beings have the ability to make choices and therefore have responsibility.*

- *Human beings are intentional, aim at goals, are aware that they cause future events, and seek meaning, value, and creativity. (http://academic.udayton.edu/jackbauer/ Readings%20595/Hum%20Psy%205%20principles.pdf).*

3.4. Transpersonal Psychology

Transpersonal Psychology represents the person and the personality as a cumulation/ overlapping of personalities, persons and universal, ancestral or cosmic values, highlighting in particular the transcendental, ancestral and spiritual content and, valences and resources of the human personality (D.H. Lajoie & S. I. Shapiro, 1992).

In transpersonal psychology are used especially terms, concepts, ideas as:

- spiritual evolution;
- religious conversion;
- altered states of consciousness;
- spiritual practices;
- spiritual self-development;
- self beyond;
- the ego;
- systemic trance;
- spiritual crises;
- peak experiences;
- mystical experiences (R. Anderson, 2011; D.H. Lajoie & S. I. Shapiro, 1992).

Regarding the specifics of therapy the authors and therapists emphasize that its goals include both traditional outcomes, such as symptom relief and behavior change, as well as action at the transpersonal level, which may transcend psychodynamic issues (R. Walsh, F. Vaughan, 1993).

3.5. Positive Psychology

Positive psychology, relatively new field of academic study, launched with the first its summit taking place in 1999 and the first *International Conference on Positive Psychology* taking place in 2003, is considered either an autonomous science, either a part of the humanistic psychology, either an extension of humanistic psychology. Probably all the affirmations are valid.

The basic premise of positive psychology is that human beings are often, perhaps more often, drawn by the future than they are driven by the past (Seligman, 2002). Essentially, this kind of psychology highlight the importance in the human life, personality and therapy or counseling of some issues and resources as:

- happiness;
- positive emotions;
- orientation to the future;
- positive expectation;
- love;
- appreciation;
- empathy;
- states of pleasure or flow;
- values;
- strengths;
- virtues, talents;
- positive experiences;
- enduring psychological traits;
- positive relationships;
- positive institutions. etc.

Seligman and Csikszentmihalyi (2000) define positive psychology as the scientific study of *positive* human functioning and flourishing on multiple levels that include the biological, personal, relational, institutional, cultural, and global dimensions of life.

3.6. The Humanistic Approach to Personality and Person

In psychology the term/ concept *Personality* is used primarily to refer to the ensemble of constant psychological and behavioral characteristics of an individual, of a concrete/ determined person, highlighting, with preference, the aspects of invariability and unity of the behavior in different situations.

Some definitions make reference to the dominance/ consistency of certain features, traits, qualities, especially from the temperament and character spheres, in the personal structure and constitution of an individual (Allport, 1961; Maslow, 2011).

Other acceptations highlight the importance of the self/ ego as core/ central instances and formations in the internal structure and functioning/ economy of personality (Friedman & Schustack, 2010; McAdams, 2009). This orientation is called as well *ego-psychology*.

Depending on the perspective of approaching, or other criteria, in psychology were outlined few major paradigms, theories, and models of personality, among which we note:

- The humanistic paradigm (C. Rogers, G. Allport, R. May, A. Maslow, V. Frankl, H. Murray, etc.);

- The psychodynamic and analytical theory (S. Freud, C. Jung, A. Adler, J. Lacan, etc.);

- The functionalist and behaviorist paradigm (W. James, B.-F Skinner, E. Thorndike, J. Dollard, N. Miller, etc.);

- The structuralist and typological paradigm (R. Cattell, H. Eysenck, K. Leonhard, A. Liciko, W. Sheldon, E. Kretschmer, etc.);
- The cognitive and social-cognitive theory (E. Kelly, J. Atkinson, A. Bandura, W. Mischel, etc.);

- The biological-temperamental theory (M. Zuckerman, E. Kretschmer, Mary K. Rothbart, etc.);

- The cybernetic model, the electronic-virtual model (J. Suler, N. Badler, R. Zheng, etc.), etc.

The structural-functionalist, or cognitive-behavioral approaches and guidelines, in psychology, emphasize, in formation and functioning, either the role of the body structure or the structural neuro-cognitive factors, either that of the structural societal, cultural, educational factors, representing the human personality mostly in a cybernetical way (Zheng, 2012), either as a reflection of the structure and physiology of the body or brain, or as a automatic product of the socio-cultural environment wherein was formed the personality, through learning, imitation and internalization of the dominant/ characteristic social roles and behaviors (Burkitt, 1991), which imprints itself ontogenetically as characteristic patterns of thought and conduct, thus marking constitutionally the structure, dynamics and functioning of the personality.

From these positions and perspectives of representation the personality, in the current specific activity, the psychologist/ psycho-sociologist, the educator, the manager, etc. aims to approach and solve collectively the clients' behavioral, mental, educational, economic, personal problems, to deal systematically with the social (psycho-social) structural-functional problems that, apriorically, cause them.

Instead**, the humanistic representation of personality,** proposes an existential-spiritual model/ approach, and prioritizes the role of the existential/ contextual human, inter-personal, psychosocial, empathetic and cultural factors in its *formation* and *functioning.*

If in the child rearing are important the material conditions, the HUMAN conditions are, in fact, those that contribute crucially to the formation of a humane and strong personality, of the ego, of the character, of the person as a whole, fulfilled and, socio-humanly, effective/ adaptable (Cusick, 2011, Moore, 1994).

Each of the two major spheres of the person, of the ontological-psychological sphere and of the psychological-social sphere, of the personality, and properly of the person, is the product of the interaction of the subject with specific, particular socio-humane factors, even if cannot be traced strict boundaries between them.

The contingent social-personal and socio-affective factors are crucial for the formation of the ontological-psychological sphere, while the cultural, morale conditions of learning and training are essential for the formation of the social-psychological sphere. Generally, the family, community, academic and professional climate/ environment greatly influencing the formation of personality and the person as a whole.

Thus, in a purely humanistic perspective, the human-personal, the human-social, the psycho-social (emotional, empathetic) factors are decisive in the formation and development of a strong, balanced, adaptable personality and happiness, socio-humanly integrated person.

The psychological-human (humane) characteristics of the nearest persons such as agreeability, carefulness, empathy, spirituality, their constant presence and consistency, in human, spiritual and moral terms, the human quality of the inter-personal relationships, the compathy, the social relationships as humane relationships are the constitutional and determinant factors that mark, crucially, the sense of the self, ego and personality development, the sense of the person development, the adaptability, the soulful welfare, the happiness.

Indubitable, the basic factors of the *humane/ prosocial* formation and structuration of personality are the social/ personal environments based on solidarity and empathy/ compathy, the cultural education oriented to people and values.

Ontogenetically, *the humanization* of personality and of the person as a whole, is an complex, multidimensional, emergent, holistic and integrator process that involves as crucial factors of formation especially the family and the school, being more pronounced in professionals such as teachers, social workers, artists - professionals and volunteers involved in specific activities for broad categories of people (McLaren, 2010).

The micro-community, in general, and the family, in special, are very important, even crucial, in the formation, functioning and beingness of the person.

In this sense, any social group, community or organization is, so, a compathetic community as well. Many human sufferings, tragedies or social problems are rooted in its underdevelopment, in weaknesses or serious compathetic problems.

The knowledge of this aspect by the educator (parent, teacher, caregiver, etc.) is a necessity and, moreover, the compathy, the empathetic community, the social-humane/ humane system of sympathies and empathies can be very effective tools for the personality formation/ development (Moore, 1994).

The empathetic community and compathy are build and specifically define through the common, collective, inter-/ trans-personal emotional, affective, sentimental, cognitive circumstances, characteristics and behaviors of the individuals who compose it. So, these consist mainly of three types of sub-processes or phenomena:

> emotional/ affective/ sentimental,

> cognitive/ intellectual, and

> spiritual/ cultural/ moral.

In this perspective each member of a community is, inter alia, a product of a unique and but also of a common, collective interaction, depending on the personality of the others, place, time, cultural niche, hazard. Every person being actually part of a particular compathetic system. This is, in turn, part of a comprehensive system. The most common compathetic system and most consistent is the family.

Into any micro-community, into the family, the compathetic consistency is given by the fact that the individual's personalities are composed of common emotional, cognitive, and cultural experiences, by the fact that in each individual personality exists, through empathy and projection, the others. It is established a mutual existential dependence between the persons and between the persons and the community as a whole.

This compathy, empathetic community works, through the organizational culture, also as a system of symbols or values that are rooted in the individual's personality or activism. These symbols and values are imposed as links and unitary resorts between the two parties. Their existence and operation give the sense of belonging, familiar, known, give comfort, safety and happiness.

Between the empathetic community and the individuals which it constitutes it is established a ontological-socio-human balance, an existential and functional optimum, in which is satisfied, in principle, in a harmonious and non-confrontational way, both the personal and the collective necessities. The empathetic community and the compathy can also have a negative influences, may be an area of non-value, of conflict, hostility or social exclusion, or can have a coherent organization and functioning but founded on non-value, on antisocial attitudes, or may be poorly organized, dysfunctional, immature. In both cases, the members are exposed to personal/ humane/ spiritual under-development, marginalization and social/ moral maladjustment.

The optimal condition for the construction and functioning of a strong, developed, equilibrate personality, a adaptable and happiness person, are the ones opposites, namely positive, functional compathy, social/ human solidarity, unity, communication, cooperation, in the family, community, organization etc. (Cusick, 2011)

The culture offers both an axiological model, but represents also an inexhaustible reservoir of spiritual and epistemological resources in the processes of forming of the superior formations and spheres of the person/ personality, mostly of the social-personal sphere, of the social ego, of the conscience and character.

Religion, morals and education, as well, through their psychological-axiological dimensions and contents (beliefs, convictions attitudes, knowledge etc.), but also through the ones social/ moral (rituals, ethics rules, etc.) can be considered important spiritual and ethical factors/ sources in the ontogenetic process of forming personality (A. F. C. Wallace, 1980).

The role of the culture, religion morals, and education being so more important in the formation, beingness and functioning of the latter one, of the social-personal / psychological-social sphere because these provide models, values, knowledge, cultural and moral frames of forming and developing.

Therefore, principally, the humanistic conception upon the formation of human personality is given by the idea that this is ontogenetical products of some gradual and stadial processes held with the crucial contribution of the biological and intellectual factors, but very important role and contribution have the axiological and moral factors, the concrete/ contextual/ contingent socio-cultural factors where the person grows and lives, mainly the moral-humane factors, with the crucial contribution of the moral conducts of the individual persons, concrete people from the proximate environment with intense and constant psychological-moral presence and influence, especially the significant members from its family/ significant group.

Essentially, the humanistic representation of personality is imposed, after our observation, through *two main approaches/ paradigms/ theories*, it is about

> *the humanistic-existential/ positive) approach/ paradigm/ theory* (Carl Rogers, Abraham Maslow, Rollo May, and others.), and

> *the humanistic-spiritual/ ontological approach/ paradigm/ theory* (Viktor Fankl, Abraham Maslow, Thomas Plante, and others),

speaking, therefore, on the one part, of a

> *psychology of the ego, consciousness and will,*

and, on the other part, of a

> *psychology of the spiritual self and of the soul.*

The Humanistic Existential/ Positive Approach/ Paradigm/ Theory of Personality focuses, especially, on personal development and social adaptation by using the psycho-volitional and cognitive-adaptive resources of the ego-personality, will and conscience.

It highlights and promotes personality traits and qualities such as:

> ➤ free will, liberty, autonomy, self-determination, self-realization,

> ➤ optimism, energy,

> ➤ hope, positive thinking,

> ➤ activity, consciousness, responsibility, etc.

The Humanistic-Spiritual/ Ontological Approach/ Paradigm/ Theory of Personality highlights especially the inner-ontological psychological-spiritual and psychological-humane content/ valence/ dimension of the personality, of the spiritual self, of the soul, their aesthetic, playful, moral or religious resources. The humanistic-ontological psychological perspective on the personality gives, as is natural, so, to the ontological-spiritual sphere the primary etiological, structural and existential role in formation, structure, beingness and functioning of the person. It highlights and promotes personality traits and qualities such as:

> ➤ spirituality, virtue,

> ➤ humanity/ humanness, altruism,

> ➤ empathy, love,

> ➤ faith, etc.

Rogers affirms that, from the humanistic psychology's position the essential and structural instance and structure of the personality is *the self*. He says that the self is an important part of the human existence and experience, and the goal of the personality training and development of each individual should be to determine/ facilitate the client to become *truly him-self* by expressing and developing its inner biological, psychological and spiritual potential, its own authentic self (Rogers, 1980).

Maslow, in the book "Toward A Psychology of Being", published in 1962, reprinted in 2011, indicates an important gap in the academic/ scientific psychology theory and methodology, namely the relatively lack in the scientific representation of the structure and composition of the personality of its ontological-spiritual content, of its *being.*

In this context he envisaged that the future of psychology, implicitly of psychotherapy, also of other areas of the social practices (education, social work, management, etc.) will depend, to a large extent, to the concerns and performances of redefining the human personality theory/ model/ paradigm, where to the ontological-spiritual and human dimension/ sphere will have to be given much more attention.

3.7. Strong/ Developed Personality

In relation to the two (humanistic) paradigms, perspectives of representation and approach, one can speak also of two spheres, forms, names, kinds of personality:

> ➢ Strong/ Developed Personality, and

> ➢ Spiritual and Humane Personality.

The first is related to the term

> ➢ Personal-Psychological Development,

and the second, to the term

> ➢ Spiritual and Humane Development.

The humane and spiritual personality and development, and the strong/ developed personality and development are complementary, interdependent, and cannot be conceived only together.

Regarding the term/ concept **Strong/ Developed Personality** it refers especially to the psychological-proactive and socio-adaptive quality, valence, dimension of the global personality, of the person as a whole, especially in social and professional context (Schellhamme, 2012).

Speaking about strong/ developed personality, in opposition to weak undeveloped personality are brought in the foreground dominant traits like:

- personal development;
- high capacity to self-determination;
- high resilience;
- high capacity to control the emotions;
- high degree of awareness, self-knowledge, self-esteem;
- high level of personal and social autonomy;
- high level of interpersonal development;
- adaptability, mature personality:
- activism and initiative;
- assertiveness, etc. (Erikson, 1998; Rogers, 1980; Maslow, 1993).

3.8. Personal Development

The Personal Development, or the Psychological-Personal Development of an individual human being is closely determined by the level of development of the strong/ developed personality, but also of the global personality or of the person as a whole, especially represented as a social being, imply, with predilection, aspect such as:

- Personal and social efficiency (Rogers, 1977, 1980);
- Socio-emotional development, control of emotions, emotional intelligence (Erikson, 1998);
- Realism and balance (Frankl, 1967);

- Powerful will, resistance to failure and frustrations (Schellhamme, 2012);

- Hope, orientation to future. positive attitude, optimism, active thinking (Seligman, 2002);

- High degree of awareness, self-knowledge, self-esteem (Maslow, 2011);

- Professional development (Erikson, 1998);

- Personal and social autonomy (Schellhamme, 2012);

- Interpersonal development (Erikson, 1998);

- Mature personality, adaptability (Rogers, 1980; Maslow, 1993).

Therefore, essentially, the humanistic-existential/ positive paradigm/ theory of personality and person, originated in existential and positive (phenomenological) philosophy, focuses specifically on personal development and social adjustment through the use of the psycho-volitional, psycho-intellectual and behavioral-adaptive resources, highlighting, therefore, its existential and socio-adaptive dimension and valence, the freedom and responsibility, the free will of the person existing in social context and action/ activity (Allport, 1961, 560; Snyder & Lopez, 2006).

This humanistic paradigm emphasizes, consequently, personality traits and qualities such as:

- activism,
- self-determination,
- freedom-accountability,
- optimism,
- energy,
- free will,
- self-realization,
- hope, active consciousness,
- personal development,
- social adaptability,

- assertiveness,
- resilience,
- happiness etc. (Seligman and Csikszentmihalyi, 2000; Schellhamme, 2012; Seligman, 2002, 99).

As was suggested above the really strong personality and personal development cannot be conceived, with some exceptions, without spiritual and humane development, the humane and spiritual personality and development, and the strong personality and development are complementary, interdependent, and cannot be conceived only together.

3.9. Spiritual and Humane Personality

The humanistic-ontological approach to personality and person highlights especially the human-spiritual and transpersonal dimension/ content, valence and resources of personality (Cortright, 1997, 123).

In this paradigm a central place is held by what it is called, especially in spiritual psychology, transpersonal psychology, humanitarian thought and movement, also in humanistic social work, **Spiritual and Human Personality**.

Speaking of spiritual and humane personality one make reference:

1. to a set of personality's formations, such as soul, spiritual self, humane consciousness, humane character, and others - structural onto-psychological and intellectual sources of the person's humane and spiritual qualities;

2. to the spiritual-humanitaristic orientation, quality, the overall humane valence, dimension of the global personality, meaning kindness, goodness, altruism, personality opened to the overall manhood jouissance, increased sensitivity to the other's suffering/ tragedy -

itself, but also emergent resource of empowerment, wellbeing and happiness for the people from ambience.

Both being foundations and explanations of the professional's humane and spiritual qualities, of its humane, altruistic, prosocial behavior in humanistic therapy, social work, education, management, art, etc.

Therefore, the complex and complete meaning of the concept *spiritual and humane personality* includes the both approaches, determining superior valences (qualities/ resources) of the person/ personality/ conduct, such as virtue, humanity, authentic happiness, etc. (P. Harvey, 1995).

Starting from our topic of the book, focused on the humanistic approach in psychotherapy, social work, and education, management and art, regarding the professionals from these practical domains we will paid particular attention to the psychological-humane and psychological-spiritual qualities and resources, of course all in the context of the global personality, of the person as a whole.

To this end, we can consider that the psychological-ontological sphere of the humane personality, especially the soul has a primordial role in determining the empathy, compathy and spiritual welfare, spirituality as personality quality, the motivational-eudaimonical sphere has a primordial role in determining the happiness and eudemonic-altruistic energy/ motivation of the person/ professional, anf the axiological-moral/ prosocial sphere has a primordial role in determining qualities of the person such as personal development, humane development and humanity of the person/ professional.

All in the context in which every trait, quality, resource of the personality is also an effect of system, and gains significance only in socio-behavioral context.

Into the psychological-ontological sphere of the (spiritual/ humane) personality an important role plays the *altruistic and spiritual jouissance,* that involves the jouissance related to higher, humane development of the personality, and the jouissance oriented towards the good/ well-being of the other, general other.

3.10. The Spiritual and Humane Development

Regarding the concept of **Spiritual and Humane Development** of the person, the aspect is highlighted by reference to two issues which involves, on the one hand, the level of development of the spiritual and human personality, and on the other hand, of the internal structure, organization of the global personality, respectively:

1. Personality developed at a higher level, the most high, the most close to the condition of human being as autonomous cultural, rational, spiritual existence, with its characteristic attributes - morality, virtue, sociality, spirituality, personal development, adaptability and socio-human efficiency, and

2. Personality structured through the soul, ego, conscience, character, motivation, skills, etc. so that determines conducts oriented towards the wellbeing of the generalized other, towards the common good, humanity, and dominant traits such as empathy, altruism, generosity, kindness, etc.

Therefore, making a synthesis, this humanistic paradigm emphasizes, consequently, spiritual and human/ humane personality traits and qualities such as:

- spirituality,
- humanity,
- empathy,
- altruism,
- generosity,
- kindness,
- morality,

- virtue,
- sociality,
- love, attachment,
- cultural and moral adaptability, etc. (P. Harvey, 1995; Schellhamme, 2012).

3.11. Humanistic Psychotherapy and Counseling

Humanistic Psychotherapy and Counseling bring in the forefront of knowledge, evaluation and therapeutic action/ activity terms, concepts, values, techniques and ideas such as:

- personality psychotherapy and counseling;
- empathy as core resource of change and empowerment;
- psychological-personal development and empowerment;
- ethical responsibility;
- self-actualization;
- client's intern potential;
- person/ client-centered-intervention;
- existential psychotherapy and counseling;
- gestalt psychotherapy and counseling;
- group psychotherapy and counseling;
- transpersonal psychotherapy;
- spiritual psychotherapy and counseling;
- the humanization of the client;
- the spiritualization of the client;
- positive psychotherapy and counseling;
- morality;
- virtue;

- sociality, love, attachment, etc. (Rogers, 1959), 1977), 1980; Maslow, 1993, 2011, Frank, 1967, etc.).

In theory and practice the humanistic psychotherapy and counseling are dominant two great directions/ modalities/ approaches:

- existential (positive, phenomenological, etc.), and

- spiritual (humane, ontological, etc.).

The existential directions/ modalities/ approaches focuses on the inner capacity of the self-determination of person/ client, on free will and self-realization, where the evaluation and intervention are based too to the research and identification of the client's existential anxieties and crisis, its internal-ontological imbalances, the rehabilitation being made through personal/ human growth and emancipation/ empowerment (Horner & Kindred, 1997).

The spiritual (humane, ontological, etc.) approaches would include, comprises, certainly, the humanistic psychotherapy as enshrined it practically, and not declarative, but it is not limited to this, it exceeds, completes and fulfills through the interest and focus on the person as spirit, as a spiritual and humane personality, with curative emphasis on the ontological-psychological interior disorders and affectations, as well as on the compathetical, inter-personal, social, cultural resorts that determine, ontogenetically, structurally, functionally and existentially, the client's disorders, affectations, problems, underdevelopments, etc.

Through the humane and spiritual personality the person/ client is formed, works and exists as part of a compathetical community of attachments, values, persons, humane relationships, and, in conclusion, the "health" of its personality and behavior is conditioned by the humane quality of this community.

In this regard, the evaluation in the humanistic-ontological paradigm of the person/ client, seeks to identify and diagnose, mostly, the structural-functional and situational disorders of the client related to its humane and spiritual development and beingness as part of a compathetical relationship and/ or community.

Also, it is important to realize an inventory of the motivational system of the customer where to highlight the more pronounced deviations from the normality of the system of needs, motives and aspirations by reference to a motivational-humane and spiritual optimum (S. Strack, 2005).

The humanistic-spiritual therapy has, so, inter alia, this first curative/ recuperative/ ameliorative task, in the process of intervention, to operate/ determine those compathetical, humane improvements at the level of inter-personal relationship, group, organization, family, couple, etc. that would lead, through the humanizing force that exercise the socio-human/ humane relationships and the humanistic group upon the person, to beneficial improvements in the internal ontological-psychological condition/ economy/ jouissance of the person (Stolorow, 2011).

3.12. Methodological Specifics

The humanistic methodology in psychotherapy uses the human personality as core resources and values with priority in the objectives regarding the personal-psychological rehabilitation and socio-human integration of the client, where the therapist, with his humane and developed global personality and behavior, succeeds to have a greater efficiency, both in the objectives involving the psychological welfare and happiness of the client, as well as in those pursuing his empowerment, autonomization, socio-human integration.

The clinical process starts with the demarche of evaluation through the representation of the client as *ego* and *complex personality*. That is why it is necessary the settlement, in the front-plan of the evaluative panel, of the dysfunctional elements and deviations from a so-called normality in the psychological-personal, humane and spiritual development/ wellbeing of the client, evaluated in the context of some systems of human/ social relationships more or less humane/ pro-humane or organizationally developed (Frankl, 1967).

In his clinical activity, through his strong/ humane personality and behavior, the therapist can contributes crucially to the achievement of the humanistic established objectives, mostly those related to the human and spiritual wellbeing of the client, to the reduction/ relieving the sufferings and anguishes, but also those concerning the empowerment, autonomization, the social, socio-humane integration and adaptation in the community where the client lives.

In this respect, the main role of the humanistic therapist is to contribute, also with the resources of his personality, of his qualities and behaviors, to the changing and transformation of the client's dehumanized and weak/ vulnerable personality in strong/ developed personality.

From the humanistic methodology and praxeology perspective the efficiency of intervention is high especially when it is considered the direct therapeutic relationship between the therapist and the client (Horner & Kindred, 1997).

Especially through the empathetic capacity and resources of his personality the therapist acquires access to the client's personality and its inner psychological experience, and, also, acquires an effective method/ way of psychological/ humane/ spiritual change/ rehabilitation/ empowerment.

This is one of the reasons why the therapist's humanity, spirituality and force/ character become important sources of change, efficiency and achievement of the methodology that it choose with the aim to achieve the assumed humanistic objectives, the psychological and social change, rehabilitation and empowerment of the client.

3.13. The Client and the Therapist

In humanistic psychotherapy and counseling of the **the client** is, firstly, a person affected existentially, structurally, functionally and situationally, in his psychological-personal, humane and spiritual personality and beingness.

Therefore, what would be *problem* and *object of intervention* is, therefore, the existential, structural, functional and situational impairment in his personal, humane and spiritual development and beingness, as well as the psychological and/ or behavioral impairment/ disturbance determined by the internal (psychological-ontological) and external (relational, compathetical) interpersonal, humane and spiritual factors.

Therefore, the epistemological foundation in the representation of the client, in the humanistic perspective, it is, in fact, its approach as person, personality, spiritual being, existing in a complex socio-humane, compathetical system/ community (Frankl, 1976).

Therefore, it is required the settlement, in the forefront of the intervention strategies, of the objective of satisfying his psychological-personal and humane and spiritual needs, together with the objective of his recovery/ stimulation and development through the compathetical community and system of interpersonal relationships.

In relation to the two (humanistic) paradigms, perspectives of representation and approach to personality, one can speak of two types of values and resources of the client's personality in humanistic therapy practice.

It is about values and resources of his *humane and spiritual personality*, on the one hand, and of his *strong, developed personality*, on the other hand.

The first is related to the term *humane and spiritual development/ resources* of the client's personality, and the second to the term *personal-psychological development/ resources* of the client's personality.

The syntagma client's *humane and spiritual personality* refers mainly to the psychological-humane and spiritual content/ nature of the client's personality, also to the humanistic orientation, quality, the overall humane and spiritual valence, dimension of the client's global personality.

The level of the client's *humane and spiritual development,* as *source and resource of resilience and recovery*, is closely determined by the level of development of his humane and spiritual personality.

The client's *strong/ developed personality* refers mainly to the proactive orientation, quality, valence, dimension of the client's global personality, meaning powerful will, resistance to failure and frustrations, interpersonal development, positive attitude, optimism, active thinking, sociability, realism and balance, high degree of awareness, self-knowledge, self-esteem etc. (Maslow, 2011).

Essentially, the strong/ developed client's personality, as value and resource in humanistic psychotherapy practice, is revealed by two key features, namely:

- client's personality developed at higher level, the most high, the most close to the condition of social being, person, as autonomous individual in community, society, group work etc., and

- client's personality structured through the ego, conscience, character, motivation, skills, etc. so that determines adaptive, efficient traits and conducts.

In this sense, therefore, the client's *personal development,* as *source and resource of resilience and recovery*, is closely determined by the level of development of its strong, psychological personality, but also of its personality as a whole, implying traits as high degree of awareness, self-knowledge, social efficiency, emotional intelligence, realism and balance, powerful will, resistance to failure and frustrations, active and positive thinking, professional development, personal and social autonomy, interpersonal development, mature personality, adaptability, etc. (Stefaroi, 2009).

Regarding the **therapist**'s personality and person it is interesting to note the aspect that the humanistic psychotherapy theory and axiology does not promote a unilateral representation of the therapist, of its qualities and conducts, even if, looked, for example, from the structuralist-functionalist and scholar perspective to humanistic approach can be reproached the exaggerated interest for the psychological-existential and psychological-ontological, spiritual and humane aspects, valences, qualities, at the expense of scientific training and professional rigor.

In reality, humanistic psychotherapy and counseling, as suggests also the origins of the term *humanism*, in which to the knowledge and science are given a privileged role, closely linked to the idea of human rights, emancipation and affirmation, promotes the scientific training, and, in conclusion, multilateral and complex, of the professional; one of the reasons being the fact that only a complex, deep and accurate knowledge of the socio-human, economic, cultural and spiritual issues of the client can facilitate an effective entry in compathetical and eudemonic-curative congruence with the humane personality and resources, with the psychological-spiritual energies of the therapist (Stefaroi, 2012).

In this regard, the therapist's personality, in the perspective of the theory, axiology and methodology of humanistic psychotherapy, is a psychosocial and cultural construction of very high complexity, gathering, ontogenetically, the natural datum with the education/ training, the internal resources with the life and professional experience.

The therapist's personality is, thus, metaphorically speaking, a huge reservoir of energy, knowledge, attitudes, feelings and habitudes with which to work to achieve the two main goals of the practice:

- empowerment, autonomization, rehabilitation and social integration, and

- reduction the sufferings, the happiness, the restoring of the human dignity of the person in difficulty and/ or pain, of the client.

In humanistic psychotherapy, which aims the psychological-personal rehabilitation and socio-human integration of the client, the issue relating the therapist's personality is of great importance, that's why it requires a comprehensive approach. The model of representation is, therefore, opposed to the behavioral-functionalist model.

The humanistic perspective on the therapist operates with a concept, of professional personality, of existential-positive and humane-spiritual type, which combines, dialectically, the humane and spiritual dimension with the one pragmatical (Maslow, 1993).

That's why, also in the process of training the therapists, is put accent on an applied spiritual-humanistic curriculum (Horner, Kindred, 1997), the aim is that of training and cultivation of the complex professional humane personality, the ability to resonate to the concrete feelings and experiences of the customers.

Strong/ developed personality, empathy, spiritual welfare, humane development and spiritual sensitivity are crucial, indispensable traits of the professional in humanistic psychotherapy. These crucial interpersonal qualities and resources, involved in the therapeutic practice, have, mainly, as we have seen, the main psychological-ontological source in its strong and humane personality.

In relation to the two main humanistic paradigms, perspectives of representation and approach to personality, ontological and existential-positive, one can speak of two types of values and resources of the professional's personality in humanistic psychotherapy. It is about values and resources of his *humane and spiritual personality*, and values and resources of his *strong/ developed global personality*.

The *humane and spiritual professional's personality* refers mainly to his psychological-ontological humane and spiritual content/ nature, also to the humanistic orientation, quality, the overall humane and spiritual valence, dimension of his global personality, meaning kindness, altruism, increased sensitivity to the other's sufferings etc. - itself, but also emergent resource of empowerment, wellbeing and happiness for the client, being foundations and explanations of the professional's humane and spiritual qualities and conducts, of his humane, altruistic, prosocial behavior in humanistic therapy.

The professional's *humane and spiritual development,* as *professional resources in the practice with the clients*, is closely determined by the level of development of his *humane and spiritual personality.*

Through the great development of the professional's humane and spiritual personality his (professional) behavior is reformed and is defined through solidarist-humanistic psychological-professional qualities and conducts such as agreeableness, tolerance, humanity etc. - core resources in working with the clients in humanistic psychotherapy practice.

The *strong/ developed professional's personality*, as resource in humanistic therapy, designates the orientation, quality, valence, dimension of the his global personality, meaning powerful will, resistance to failure and frustrations, interpersonal development, positive attitude, optimism, active thinking, communicativity, sociability, realism and balance, high degree of awareness, self-knowledge etc. In this sense, the *professional's efficiency/ resources* in practice is closely determined by the level of development of the strong/ developed (psychological-personal) personality, but also of his personality as a whole.

The great professional characters, dedicated to the good of the clients, incorporate, in a sublime manner, both the spiritual/ humane development and the psychological-personal development, thus ensuring, besides a consistent internal spiritual/ humane personal functionality and a high external professional functionality/ efficiency (Shebib, 2002; Maslow, 1993).

3.14. Person-Centered Psychotherapy/ Counseling

The person-centered psychotherapy and counseling are linked especially to the name of Carl Rogers.

Through the person/ client-centered therapy/ psychotherapy, the person/ client-centered counseling, or the rogerian psychotherapy as it is also called, Rogers (1951) has the crucial merit to be worked to the foundation of the modern psychotherapy as a whole, also through the *non-directive* therapeutic-humanistic methods and values promoted in theory and practice, with large application also in education, social work and other domain of the socio-human practices and activities.

The core idea of the established client-centered therapy, promoted by Rogers and developed by followers, is that, in the therapeutic process must to take the client's accounts seriously, because he, his personality is the basis for helping and healing, by finding his inner resources, in his personality and concrete (circumstantial) socio-human relationships.

In this sense the therapist can use the internal circumstantial experiences of the client as resources in the process of rehabilitation, empowerment, normalization.

Today, the person/ client-centered therapy is known and applied by considering the following aspects:

- the therapist must accept the client unconditionally, without judgment, disapproval or approval;

- the therapist experiences an empathic understanding of the client's internal frame of reference;

- the therapist helps the client to believe that the therapist has an unconditional love for them;

- the psychotherapist/ counselor must manifest increased trust in the client potential and in its capacity to recover, rehabilitate, grow and develop with its own resources, the role of the therapist being principally to guide it;

- the therapeutic relationship must be a relationship in which each person's perception of the other is very important;

- into the framework of the therapeutic relationship must to exist an empathetical/ compathetical congruence (emotional, cognitive etc.) between the client and therapist;

- the therapist must involve in the therapeutic relationship his own experiences to facilitate the rehabilitation, development, emancipation, empowerment of the client (Rogers, 1977).

Interpreting the person/ client-centered therapy through the humanistic ontological theory/ paradigm of the person/ client it is important to take the client's spiritual an psychological-ontological experience and live seriously, because they are the basis for helping and healing, by finding their spiritual and humane inner resources, in their humane personality and concrete human, compathetic relationships. In this end the therapist can use the internal psychological-ontological experiences of the client as resources in the process of rehabilitation, empowerment, normalization

3.15. Existential Psychotherapy/ Counseling

The existential psychotherapy an counseling focuses, especially, on aspects, objectives and approaches such as:

> the research/ identification and the solving, diminishing of the client's existential anxieties/ crisis, impasses,

> self-determination of the person/ client,

> freedom and responsibility,

> free will, and

> the search and develop of the inner client's meanings of life, etc. (Deurzen and Kenward, 2005).

This kind of therapy approaches the client as a whole and as person being, existing in situation, concrete, unique existential context using a psychological-positive/ phenomenological approach that promotes the client's inner psychological-personal, volitional capacities and aspirations, but simultaneously acknowledging its limitations and weaknesses (Yalom, 1980).

In the therapeutic process of evaluation and intervention the therapist and the client must reflect together upon how the client has answered life's questions in the past, but attention will be put to searching for a new and increased awareness in the present and enabling in conclusion a new freedom and responsibility to act.

Both, the evaluation and intervention are based on a series of philosophical-existential theses, proposing the research/ identification of the existential anxieties/ crisis and internal-ontological rebalancing/ rehabilitation through personal/ human growth and emancipation/ empowerment – solutions very useful both in evaluation as well as in intervention, especially in the practice with the clients with depression and anxiety, also with problems of adaptation and social integration (Krill, 1978).

In existential therapy and counseling, but from the humanistic ontological perspective of the person/ client, the activity seeks, inter alia, as evaluation, to research/ identification the existential-spiritual and existential-humane anxieties/ crisis, while, in intervention, it aims to achieve the internal-ontological spiritual rebalancing/ rehabilitation through spiritual growth and emancipation/ empowerment – solutions very useful in the practice with clients with depression and anxiety, with problems of adaptation and social integration, but also in the practice with clients with great problems of personal and human fulfillment (Deurzen and Kenward, 2005).

One of the most important goal of the existential therapy and counseling is that to determine the clients to find meaning and purpose in their lives and often experience heightened self-awareness, self-understanding, self-respect, and self-motivation.

3.16. Gestalt Psychotherapy and Group Psychotherapy

As was stated in theory and especially in practice the **gestalt therapy** proposes/ involves the achievement of the convergence between consciousness, experience and behavior, between the person and environment, "between the figure and the background", "here and now", from a holistic philosophical perspective.

So, this kind of therapy emphases the importance, for the client, of being aware of what it is *here and now*, and accepting the responsibility for his situation, in its psycho-social environment (Wheeler, 1991, p. 65).

Going forward, and interpreting the gestalt therapy in the humanistic-ontological perspective we say that the gestalt therapy proposes/ involves the achievement of the convergence between the client's psychological-ontological sphere, humane personality, consciousness, experience and behavior, between the person's humane personality and the socio-human community, "between the figure and background", "here and now", from a holistic philosophical-ontological and humanistic perspective.

So, the gestalt therapy, the humanistic-ontological theory/ paradigm of the person (client and therapist), emphases the importance, especially for the client, of being aware of what and how is its spiritual and humane situation and state, *here and now*, and accepting the responsibility for his existential psychological-ontological, spiritual, socio-human situation, in its psycho-social, socio-human environment (Stemberger, 2008).

In the **humanistic group psychotherapies** the (therapeutic) group are not represented as a simple bunch of persons in difficulty, but it is formed gradually as an elevated cultural, spiritual and socio-human environment, as a healer compathetical/ humane community by the unimaginable force that generates the emergence/ conmergence of the spiritual, humane energies involved.

3.17. Transpersonal and Spiritual Psychotherapy - The Humanization and Spiritualization of the Person/ Client

Transpersonal and spiritual psychotherapy seeks to explore and capitalize the profound and complex levels of the client's personality and consciousness, representing the person in general as a cumulation/ overlapping of (human and spiritual) personalities, persons and universal, ancestral or even, in some interpretations, cosmic "entities" and "values" (D.H. Lajoie & S. I. Shapiro, 1992).

In transpersonal psychotherapy are used especially terms, concepts, ideas as spiritual, transhuman and transpersonal development, spiritual and human self-development, systemic trance, spiritual crises, etc.

Regarding the specifics of this kind of therapy the authors and therapists emphasize that its goals include both traditional outcomes, such as symptom relief and behaviour change, as well as action at the transpersonal level, which may transcend psychodynamic issues.

One of the most important way of intervention in transpersonal and spiritual psychotherapy is the emancipation, empowerment and development of the client through its (re-) spiritualization and humanization, through spiritual and human/ humane empowerment and development (R. Walsh, F. Vaughan, 1993).

Even if is a very complex and difficult endeavor, the humanization, spiritualization and humane-spiritual (cosmic) integration of the person is described by the therapists, for some categories of clients, as miraculous solutions for many kinds of problems, sufferings, deviances, etc.

The therapeutic process of (re-) humanization and spiritualization starts from the observation that many of the people's disorders, sufferings, deviations and problems are caused or favored of some serious deficits of psychological-humane and spiritual development.

The therapeutic process begins, so, with what we could call spiritual-humanistic and psychological-transpersonal evaluation, that seeks to identify and diagnoses mostly the structural-functional and situational impairments of the customer relating its psychological-humane and spiritual and transpersonal development and beingness.

Therefore, the epistemological foundation of the evaluation in humanistic-spiritual and transpersonal perspective it is, actually, the representation of the client as "trans-human" personality, as spiritual, multi-dimensional, "multilayer" and transpersonal being.

That is why it is necessary the settlement, in the front-plan of the diagnostic panel, of the dysfunctional elements and deviations from a so-called normality in the transpersonal and spiritual development of the client as person and personality, with their main spheres, areas, dimensions - psychological-ontological, psychological-relational, axiological, praxeological, etc.

In the transpersonal-humanistic therapy the practitioner, through his complex and spiritual/ transpersonal personality, contributes crucially to the achievement of the humanistic established objectives, mostly those relating to the spiritual wellbeing of the client, to the reduction/ relieving the sufferings and anguishes, but also to those concerning the empowerment, autonomization, the social, socio-humane integration and adaptation in the community where the client lives.

Through its behavior, creativity and projectivity, the humanistic therapist works at the construction of a new (spiritual) *modus vivendi*, of some new (socio-human) behaviors of the customers, with humanistic-transpersonal and spiritual tools and methods.

So, with methods and behaviors of humanistic-ontological type, the therapist performs changes and re-modelings of the current psychological-spiritual, social, cultural and psychosocial situation of the client, changes and improvements in the concrete situations of depersonalization and dehumanization, in the individual and collective situations of transpersonal-existential impasses and crisis, in the client' situations of loss of the spiritual meaning in his life, and, so, to fulfill, also with the transpersonal and spiritual resources of the therapist's personality, especially through (re-) humanization and (re-) spiritualization, the constitutional objectives of the transpersonal and spiritual psychotherapy.

In this respect it is presumable that the importance of the transpersonal and spiritual qualities of the therapist to increase, the results following to highlights, especially in enhancing the activity effectiveness and achieving the objectives, where the role of these resources and qualities of the therapist to imposes almost decisive (D.H. Lajoie & S. I. Shapiro, 1992).

The researches and clinical evidences indicates that, in all the areas of the social and therapeutic practices, spirituality and humanity are some innate human capability, resource of the practitioners and clients that can be used to increase the efficiency in both the psychological-spiritual and the integrative, prosocial objectives.

In transpersonal and spiritual psychotherapy the efficiency is high especially when it is considered the direct assistential/ therapeutic relationship between the therapist and the client.

So, the therapist, with the spiritual, transpersonal capacity of his personality and behavior succeeds to have a greater efficiency, both in the objectives involving the welfare and happiness of the client, as well as in those pursuing his empowerment, autonomization, socio-human integration.

The level of development of the spiritual-empathetic capacity/ qualities of the professional, in any philosophy or theoretical orientation, form, doctrine of therapy, represents essential predictors of effectiveness and fulfillment of the objectives, the more in humanistic therapy, where this quality/ resource of the professional exceeds the original psychosocial meaning, instituting so as a core value of the efficiency in practice.

The reason is that, in the humanistic therapy practice by means of the empathetic-spiritual resources of their own personality, the professional can engage most effective the resources for spiritual, eudaimonical and social rehabilitation of the customer's personality. Spiritual, eudaimonical and social rehabilitation being core objectives and efficiency indicators of this important path of therapy (R. Anderson, 2011; D.H. Lajoie & S. I. Shapiro, 1992).

Therefore, regarding the importance of spirituality and virtue, as qualities of the professional's personality in activity effectiveness and achieving the objectives, this is given by the fact that the relationship with the client is not objectual but "spiritual", and very complex, and therefore the dominant resources involved must be of this nature.

It is, so, impossible to imagine professional efficiency, in the jobs that involve working with people in need and suffering, without spirituality, virtue, culture, with the soulful welfare and happiness state that it determines. The professionalism, in working with people, being so strongly conditioned by the level of general personal and human development, including the degree of spirituality and charisma/ virtue of the person who provide social services.

At the professionals with developed spiritual personality the spiritual sensibility and virtue will be imposed as main factors of organization and holistic adjustment of the humanistic professional behavior, becoming a crucial attribute/ source of prosocial action and effective professional practice; without virtue and spirituality the professional being under the dominion of selfishness, impulsiveness, personal undeveloped, laziness, lack of involvement, inactivity, inefficient professional behavior, dominating the defensive behaviors and non-involvement (R. Anderson, 2011).

That is one of the reasons why the therapist's virtue and spirituality becomes, in transpersonal and spiritual psychotherapy, important sources of efficiency and achievement of the assumed humanistic objectives, of psychological and social change, rehabilitation and empowerment of the people in need or suffering, of the clients (R. Walsh, F. Vaughan, 1993).

3.18. Positive Psychotherapy

Essentially, the positive psychotherapy, in evaluation and intervention, starts from the premise that human beings are often, perhaps more often, drawn by the future than they are driven by the past, using in therapeutic process of intervention especially the inner psychological-eudaimonical resources of the client, but also of the psychotherapist (Seligman and Csikszentmihaly, 2000).

Regarding the aspect of efficiency in positive psychotherapy, for example in the therapeutic work with clients in suffering, especially in the activities that involve children, elderly and persons with disabilities, the studies conclude that the efficiency, the success of intervention is strongly conditioned by the degree of happiness, enthusiasm, energy, optimism and personal charisma of the therapist.

The achievement of therapeutic goals in positive psychotherapy and counseling is so, among others, correlated with the therapist and clients's positive attitudes towards the life, with the degree of internal psychological relaxation, the irony and the personal happiness (Seligman, 2002), qualities and resources that need to be identified, promoted and developed both at the client's level but also at the therapist's level.

Therefore, more broadly, the positive psychotherapy and counseling use, in assessment and intervention, terms, ideas and resources as:

- positive emotions;

- orientation of the intervention to the future;
- the use and determination of positive experiences;

- positive expectation;

- psychological wellbeing and happiness;

- the use and determination of positive relationships;

- positive institutions;

- love, attachment, appreciation, empathy;

- states of pleasure or flow;

- values, strengths, virtues, talents, etc. (Seligman and Csikszentmihalyi, 2000; Seligman, 2002).

Concluding, essentially, the core idea of positive psychotherapy and counseling is that, in practice, the therapist and counselor aim to increase the positive feelings, the happiness, the psychological wellbeing, but also the positive behaviors and relationships, to increase also the positive cognitions but also the positive expectations, as opposed to focusing on the negative thoughts and expectations, and dysfunctional behaviors and relationships.

Chapter 4

The Humanistic Approach and Method in Sociology and Social Work

Content

The
Humanistic Approach
in
Psychology & Psychotherapy,
Sociology & Social Work,
Pedagogy & Education,
Management and Art:

Personal Development
and
Community Development

4.1. Introductory Aspects

Like psychology sociology has experienced in the second half of the twentieth century radical changes, in a large extent determined by the offensive of so-called *humanistic theory and method* in all the areas of the social sciences and practices. In the context of offensive of phenomenology and existentialism the humanistic thinking and method have manifested also in sociology, and, consequently in social work, instituting humanistic social work, in management, instituting humanistic management, and in other domains of practice that are "alimented", theoretically-methodologically, from sociology as science of the social phenomena and processes.

The same as in psychology and psychotherapy, in sociology and social work were imposed the two major orientations of the humanistic approach: *existential/ positive* and *ontological-cultural/ spiritual*.

Essentially, **the humanistic-existential (positive) direction/ theory** represents the socio-human (micro-) community through features such as strong organizational culture, high functionality, high cohesion, unity, solidity, adaptability, resilience, high autonomy, resistance to crisis and challenges, good management, etc., while **the humanistic-ontological-cultural/ spiritual approach/ theory** of community highlights ideas and features as people-centered community, dominance of the inter-personal relationships of attachment, love, respect, dominance of the practices and customs of mutual helps, social/ group/ community solidarity, harmony, unity, inter-personal congruency, socio-human, inter-personal, community functionality, socio-human, moral and cultural integration/ cohesion, the presence/ dominance of people with personality

93

and behavior traits like altruism, empathy, kindness, goodness, tolerance, understanding, charity, helpfulness etc.

Crucial concept, value and objective in sociology and social work is **community development**, reveled of features such as social and economical efficiency, high control of the processes and activities, resistance to crisis, orientation to the future. optimism, economic development, cultural development, institutional development, high autonomy, interpersonal development, high functionality, inter-community development, planning, collaboration, solidarity, democracy etc.

The humanistic-therapeutic/ assistential perspective on community, on the socio-human entities, promotes, therefore, a concept of community development where it is aimed to empower groups of people and the individuals with the skills they need to determine beneficial changes within their communities. These skills are often created through the formation of communities working for common goals.

Of the humanistic perspective, the great inclusive, cohesive, autonomous and developed communities incorporate, in a sublime manner, both the features of the organizational/ institutional development and the features of the humane, moral and cultural development, representing, in this connection, also, great values and resources in humanistic social work.

4.2. Humanistic Sociology

Humanistic Sociology is an important theoretical, heuristical, and futuristical branch of sociology, also an important source and methodological resource for humanistic social sciences and practices, for humanistic social work and humanistic management (leadership), but also for humanistic pedagogy/ education and humanistic aesthetics (theatrology, filmology, etc.).

Among the most important concerns of humanistic sociology are:

- the observation of how individuals as complex and unforeseeable human beings, as persons specifically live, love, suffer, interact;

- what attachment relationships are established between them in relationships of kinship, friendship, enmity, interest, collegiality, power relationships (C.W. Mills, 1959; Znaniecki, 1934);

- how persons and groups adjust, interactively, their behaviors and symbolizes, mutually, the social existence (the laws, values, customs, rituals, behaviors, institutions, ideologies) (Znaniecki, 1969);

- the resilience and coping with difficult situations;

- how persons and groups solve the problems;

- how persons and groups adapt to the changes or react to crisis or major events (Merton & Nisbet, 1961).

Essentially, the humanistic approach and method in sociology make the accent on human subjectivity and creativity, highlighting how individuals respond to social constraints and actively assemble social worlds, dealing with concrete human experiences, with their socio-human, inter-personal, inter-human organization. promoting a kind of society in which there is less exploitation, oppression and injustice. From the perspective of humanistic sociology's principles, the person, as being, subject, self matter and prevail in the relationships with the society as a whole and with the man as ancestral entity (C.W. Mills, 1959).

In this sense, in humanistic sociology the person is not a simple element, or a tool, means for society or humanity to achieve their objectives, the historical and ancestral goals, but, conversely, the society, the community are the existential frame where the person is fulfilled, where expresses its vocation for freedom and finds the happiness in the unique and irreducible existence and life that it has (Merton & Nisbet, 1961).

Humanistic sociology is also a militant science, this is the reason why one of the most important purposes/ directions is the study of how to make a better world, the key commitment is that *people matter* (C.W. Mills, 1959; Znaniecki, 1934).

4.3. (Humanistic) Microsociology and Psychosociology

Microsociology is a constitutional branch of sociology that, in a *humanistic* perspective, examines with priority the humane and cultural aspects of the

> ➢ the laws,
> ➢ rules,
> ➢ mores,
> ➢ customs.

of the micro-groups and particular socio-human contexts (Merton & Nisbet, 1961).

Humanistic microsociology, focuses, therefore, on the subjective/ human/ socio-human processes, on the interpersonal relationships and phenomena - of attachment, of solidarity, of love, of conflict, cooperation, etc. (Garfinkel, 2006) - crucial resources and categories in humanistic social work, humanistic management. humanistic pedagogy/ education, humanistic aesthetics (theatrology, filmology), etc..

(Humanistic) **Psychosociology** can be defined as the science that studies, among others, the cognitive and emotional, socio-human, psychological-subjective, inter-personal, inter-human, inter-psychological processes, the concrete relationships and interpersonal phenomena and processes of

- influence,
- persuasion,
- knowlwdge (social perception and representation),
- cooperation and conflict,
- attachment and love,
- conformity,
- compliance,
- obedience, etc.

An essential (humanistic) concept and category both in microsociology and psychosociology is *interpersonal attraction* (D. Bem, 1970).

In humanistic perspective the syntagm refers especially to all forces that lead people to like each other, establish relationships, and (in some cases) fall in love.

One of the most important factors in the interpersonal attractions is how similar two particular people are. The more similar two people are in general attitudes, backgrounds, environments, worldviews, etc. (G. W Allport, 1985).

4.4. Human (Humane and Strong) Relationships

In the general *humanistic* approach the syntagm **Human Relations** is used for ideas and situations such as the social and interpersonal relationships between *human* beings, the study of group behavior in order to improve the interpersonal relationships etc.

In the most socio-human relationships persons sharing similar characteristics, and often have a sense of human/ humane unity/ solidarity (Znaniecki, 1969, 94). In the humanistic approach the relations exhibit a high degree of socio-human cohesion and are more than simple links between individuals.

Generally, the concept *human relations* is as complex as vague, including a very large area of issues and topics, from the simple inter-personal relations to aspects and themes such as attachment, empathy, or complex phenomena of group or society like social solidarity and humanity. The optimal framework of their manifestations is the *micro-community* (Mayo, 1933).

The Humanistic-Spiritual/ Ontological approach to Human Relations highlights especially the ontological-humane-cultural content of the human relations, giving, as is natural, to the ontological-humane and cultural sphere the primary etiological, structural and existential role.

In this approach it is about **Humane Relationships**.

The Humanistic-Positive Approach to Human Relations originated in existential sociology, focuses specifically on the human relations development and social adjustment through the use of the adaptive resources, highlighting, therefore, the existential and cohesive dimension in the social relationships.

In this approach it is about **Strong Relationships**.

4.5. Humane Community

In relation to the two (humanistic) paradigms, perspectives of representation and approach, one can speak of two types of microcommunities. It is about of *humane and cultural microcommunity*, on the one hand, and of the *strong, developed microcommunity*, on the other hand. The first category is related to the term *humane and cultural development*, and the second to the term *organizational development*.

The sociological category/ term, syntagm *Humane Community* brings into focus issues, features such as:

- people-centered community organization and functioning;

- dominance of the inter-personal relationships of attachment, love, respect;

- dominance of the practices and customs of mutual helps;

- social/ group/ community solidarity;

- harmony, unity, inter-personal congruency;

- socio-human, inter-personal, community functionality, social integration/ cohesion;

- the presence/ dominance of people with personality and behavior traits like altruism, empathy, kindness, goodness, tolerance, understanding, charity, helpfulness etc.

The persons which live in communities with a *high degree of socio-humane development.* of socio-humane harmony, unity, inter-personal congruency, secure attachment, socio-human, inter-personal, community functionality, social integration/ cohesion develop/ adopt, consequently, attributes and qualities such as socio-human adaptability, socio-human integration, happiness, high degree of personal development, high degree of interpersonal development, high degree of social development, strong will, resistance to failure and frustration, focus on the future, optimism, active thinking, personal/social autonomy, maturity, etc. (Dominelli, 2002).

Any social group, community or organization is, in a lesser or a greater extent, a humane community. The humane community it's built and specifically functions through the common circumstances, characteristics and behaviors of the individuals that compose it. Consists mainly of three types of processes or phenomena: emotional, cognitive and spiritual.

In this perspective each member of a community is a product of a unique interaction, depending on the personality of the each other, place, time, cultural niche, hazard. Each person is actually part of a particular compathetic system. It is, in turn, part of a comprehensive system. The most common humane, compathetical system and most consistent is the family.

The compathetical/ humane consistency is given by the fact that the individual personalities are composed of common experiences, by the fact that in each individual personality exists, through empathy and projection, the others. Are established so a mutual existential dependence.

This humane community works, through the organizational culture, as a system of symbols or values as well, that are rooted. in great measure, in the individual's personality or activism. These symbols and values are imposed as links and unity resorts between the parties. Their existence and operation give the sense of belonging, familiar, known, give comfort, safety and happiness.

Between the humane/ empathetic community and the individuals is established a humane/ cultural-ontological balance, an existential and functional optimum where is satisfied, existentially, in a harmonious and non-confrontational way, both the personal and the collective necessities.

4.6. Strong Community

Essentially, the sociological syntagm, term *Strong* or *Developed Community* refers to a set of *community features* such as:

> ➢ strong institutional organization,
> ➢ strong organizational culture,
> ➢ strong economy,
> ➢ high functionality,
> ➢ strong rules and institutions and others -

- structural organizational and relational sources of the community cohesion, adaptability, resilience, assertiveness, as well as to the *proactive orientation, quality, valence, dimension* of *the global community*, of the community as entity, unity, meaning

> ➢ resistance to crisis and challenges,
> ➢ inter-communities development,
> ➢ powerful institution,
> ➢ orientation to the future,
> ➢ planification, collaboration,
> ➢ good management, etc. (Vanier, 1989, 6).

4.7. Community Development

Generally, *the community development* are closely determined by the global level of development/ organization of the global community, approaching the community, therefore, as a whole and as a social-institutional entity existing in a comprehensive, larger social/ societal context.

In humanistic perspective, a high level of community development is reveled of features such as:

- Social and economical efficiency;

- High control of the processes and activities;

- Resistance to crisis;

- Orientation to the future. optimism;

- Economical development;

- Cultural development;

- Institutional development;

- Autonomy;

- Interpersonal development;

- High functionality;

- Inter-community development;

- planification, collaboration, etc. (C.W. Mills, 1959, Merton & Nisbet, 1961).

Essentially, in a humanistic-existential/ positive paradigm/ theory of community, the community development promotes the concept of social efficiency through the use of the institutional, organizational and cultural resorts, through the ase of psychological categories and resources of the individuals which compose it as activism, self-determination, freedom-accountability, optimism, energy, self-realization, hope, active consciousness, personal development, social adaptability, assertiveness, resilience, etc.

The humanistic perspective on community, on the socio-human entities, promotes, therefore, a concept of community development where it is aimed to empower individuals and groups of people with the skills they need to effect change within their communities. These skills are often created through the formation of large social groups working for common goals (Merton & Nisbet, 1961).

The dominant conception is that, at least from the humanistic perspective, the great inclusive, cohesive and developed communities incorporate, in a sublime manner, both the features of the organizational/ institutional development and the features of the humane development of the community, representing, in this connection, great values and resources in humanistic social work or humanistic management practice.

4.8 The Humanistic Approach to Social Work

Essentially, the assumed humanistic approach/ method in social work proposes, theorizes and promotes a reaffirmation/ restatement of the fundamental/ constitutional humanistic values of social work, incorporating, in the same time, in a (relative) new coherent and unitary theory, all what penetrated in social work in the last decades, especially from humanistic psychology and psychotherapy, but also from microsociology and humanistic sociology, from human rights philosophy/ movement, etc. These being, also, among the main its theoretical sources and foundations.

As is well known, social work has experienced in the second half of the twentieth century radical changes, in important measure determined by the offensive of humanistic theory and method in all the areas of social science and practice. With old origins even in antiquity, passing through Renaissance, and then reinvigorated by phenomenology and existentialism, the humanistic thinking and method have manifested, powerfully, initially in psychology, instituting the humanistic psychology and psychotherapy, as the third way alongside psychoanalysis and behaviorism, then in pedagogy, sociology, management and other fields.

How, social work is "fed", theoretically-methodologically, largely, from these socio-human science and practice, inevitably, directly or indirectly, the humanistic values, theories and methodology it made its presence increasingly also in its specific values, theories and methodology, redimensioning and reforming them, gradually and subtly, almost entirely (M. Payne, 2011).

Despite appearances the penetration of the humanistic axiology, epistemology, and praxeology in social work, in practices, legislation, education, or literature did not on an "empty land". The humanistic ideas, methods and practices have manifested and imposed in the context of dominance of two theoretical-methodological and institutional well established systems of social work, welfare and policy, somewhat opposite and complementary, it's about, on the one hand, of traditional social work, named conventional as well, focused on individual material and financial help and care (predominantly biologically and emotionally), and the structural social work, called, depending on nuances, critical, radical, institutional as well, focused on structure, system, institution, on the projects of imposing the general welfare and social justice through fundamental structural-societal measures of change and community/ society empowerment. In philosophical-axiological and theoretical-epistemological plan the humanistic orientation in social work had, and has now, an ideational-doctrinal context dominated by schools of thought, ideas and theories like the structural-functionalist theories, learning theories, conflict theory, systems theory, psychodynamic theories etc.

However, the humanistic theory and method, with the two dominant orientations, ethical-solidarist and existential-positive, succeeded, gradually, to make place in the social work's literature, legislation and practice through values, objectives and terms such as empowerment, accountability, social justice, human and personal development, happiness, human being, human relationships etc. and to determine even a shift of emphasis from subsistence, material aid and biological-emotional basic care to humanistic-positive values and goals such as client empowerment, human rehabilitation/ development of the person and community, happiness, personal development and education for social rehabilitation and integration of people from residential institutions, especially of children.

Mutations supported by the establishment of a theoretical and methodological framework more solid and praxeologically argued by the adoption and consecration of some taken or specific theories such as attachment theory, empathy theory, the theories of human development of the person and community, the complex systems theory, the interactionist, contextualist and constructionist theories, or the care theory, redimensioned by focusing on the humane side of the care, on empowerment and self-determination, and of some methods and practices, largely taken from the humanistic psychotherapy, such as the client-centered methods/ practices, the existential methods, the gestalt methods etc.

The effective establishment of the declared humanistic theory, method and practice in social work has led, logically, to the affirmation as well of a specific title: Humanist Social Work - phrase that tends to adjoin to the more consecrated traditional social work and structural social work. What particularizes the humanistic social work, in addition to the system of specific values and methods/practices, is the human/ humane, humanistic-positive system of resources, which must, ultimately, to generate the change, the empowerment, the human rehabilitation and the reintegration.

If traditional social work operates mainly with material and "emotional" resources, and structural/ critical social work with institutional, ideological and juridical-political resources (Allan, (Pease & Briskman, 2003) humanistic social work promotes as resources and values, at the same time, on the one hand, the human personality, the person, the individuality, the self/ ego, the soul, the character, the skills, the will and the conduct, of the client and of the professional, and, on the other hand, the human, inter-human, inter-personal relationships, of group, community, the human relations lesser understood as mere social relations and mostly as humane relationships, generators of empowerment, human-psychological, personal development and happiness - resources for whose use the professionals and the services appeal to ways of empowerment such as the empathy, the inter-empathy, the transfer, the psycho-social influence etc. (Stefaroi, 2012).

4.9. Humanistic Social Work – Core Theoretical Issues

As philosophy and theory, humanistic social work is a conglomerate of theories, paradigms, orientations, but it have some crucial ideas, principles, values as vectors:

- emphasis on the client's and the professional's personality, on the human/ humane relationships and micro-community, as basic resources of practice;

- the universal human/ person rights;

- social justice;

- a humanistic perspective on the practitioner, on his qualities and conducts in practice;

- the person/ client represented as *human* being, with sentiments, soul, personality, desires, sufferings, needs of love, needs of happiness and accomplishments;

- positive, optimistic and appreciative expectation in practice, person-centered and community-centered approach in evaluation and intervention;

- concentration, in the activities of recuperation, integration on the present and the future and less on the past;

- emphasis especially on durable change and less on momentary help, aid, etc.

Social work, in general, theoretically and methodologically, is based on the resources of social and human sciences, philosophy and other areas of the science and practice (Howe, 2009).

This is one of the reasons why the theory and practice of social work are so complex and full of dichotomies and doctrinal or methodological contradictions, taking, so, from these the majority theories and tools of practice, but, too, the theoretical/ doctrinal debates regarding the relationships between the structure and agency, individual and society, freedom and responsibility, matter and spirit, structure and element, individualism and solidarity, stagnation and change (through evolution vs. revolution), the issue of individual and collective rights, etc.

Practically, the theory and practice of social work comes from behind, from the past, assimilating them, usually afterwards, and adapting them to the specific purpose, mission and methods (Goroff, 1981).

Thus, these determines the specific epistemology and methodology of social work to include, harmonious or dichotomous, orientations, ways, perspectives and theories of the whole areas of the contemporary philosophy and socio-human sciences: phenomenologist, existentialist, feminist, post-modern, structuralist, behaviorist, psychoanalytic, psychosocial, cognitivist, holist, functionalist, criticist, traditionalist, radical, constructivist, humanist, etc. (Payne, 2005).

Yet, at a first glance, social work, as theory and practice, is dominated by two, relatively opposed, major ways, forces, orientations, namely Traditional or Conventional Social Work and Radical or Critical Social Work. The theoretical and doctrinal debate between the two constitutes subject of many books, articles and studies.

Traditional or Conventional Social Work is based, axiological-doctrinal and methodological, predominantly on the humanistic-traditionalist values and practices regarding the relationship between the individual welfare and the public welfare, with an important religious origin and support.

Essentially, this tradition involves that the society, community have a moral responsibility, unconditioned, toward the person in need, in suffering; situations that places it into ta hypostasis under the ancestral condition of human being and, consequently, the society, community, family must intervene to normalize its social and human situation, mainly through material support and care (physical and emotional), without having in focus structural interventions. to change from the ground the systemic conditions that generate or maintain the problem.

According to many authors it is the starting point in any theoretical and ideological discussion regarding the values, mission and methods of the social work, both of chronological and axiological-methodological considerations, for the simple reason that it is the first and original form, but also because it provides the fundamental system of values and purposes of the social work/ welfare practice.

Helping and caring the peoples being in difficulty and/or suffering, human/ social solidarity, redistribution, sensibility for the other's welfare are universal values and objectives of the social work, anytime and anywhere.

Biestek (1978), defines traditional social work especially through some key values and principles such as:

- First the agency and then the structure;

- Focusing on the person's distress (physical and emotional);

- Individualization;

- Acceptance, tolerance and nondiscrimination;

- Non-judgmental attitude;

- Confidentiality and respect for client as a person.

So, Traditional Social Work is less interested in the social, economic or political context, which determines or support the social problems, or in the structural socio-political progress or change, which could lead to the elimination or reducing the problems, the focus is, so, on the needs and feelings of the individuals/ clients, considering each client as a unique person, each individual must to be treated as a unique human being and not just as a structural member of a community, group or society.

The traditional social work practice is much indebted to the civic sense of people, sense of unity and appurtenance to the human species, to the specific moral and religious practices and values from the religion or culture in which it applies.

The care theories, helping theories, social solidarity theories, and humanitarian theories, mainly, underlying the traditional or conventional social work's epistemology, methodology and practice. The practitioners meet, with preference, the roles of caregiver, counselor/ therapist, facilitator, broker and evaluator.

Critical and/or Radical Social Work were established and affirmed as critical responses la the Traditional Social Work. Traditional Social Work, as practice and method, being accused of an attitude of condescension and contempt towards its clients, while the traditional social worker being considered an indispensable tool of the ruling classes from capitalist society (Bailey and Brake, 1975).

In this sense, the promoters of Radical and/or Critical Social Work states that the undeclared mission of the Traditional Social Work is, in fact, to contribute at the maintaining of the capitalist state order, and therefore, at the chronic social and economic polarization, at the chronic institutionalized, systematic oppression, social injustice and other chronic/ structural societal anomalies.

Regarding the theoretical-philosophical sources and support, to a large extent, the modern and scientific thought and methods, the critical and radical theories, the theories of social change and progress (hegelian, marxist, structuralist, feminist, etc), the anti-discriminatory and anti-oppressive theories, the post-colonial and new-structural theories underlying, epistemologically and methodologically, this paradigm/ paradigms of social work/ welfare.

The main purpose of the Radical and/or Critical Social Work is to move away from the traditional approaches, that were based on a medical and emotional model of the man, that places people in a passive position, with the focus on the person (especially on the material and emotional needs) rather than on the society and community as a whole, on the structural and systemic level, from where, according to the theoreticians of Radical and Critical Social Work, derived the social and human problems (Mullaly, 2006).

Thus, through its constitutional nature Radical/ Critical Social Work is established as a response and critical attitude, even revolutionary, against traditional/ conventional social work, promoting values, categories or practices such as:

- First the structure and then the agency;
- Focusing on the community and structural changes;
- Community and society empowerment;
- Social change;
- Structural and systemic social work;
- Progressive social work;
- Social justice;
- Anti-oppression policies;
- Radical reforms, etc.

If Traditional/ Conventional Social Work focuses the concern on the person welfare, here and now, in Critical/ Radical Social Work the emphasis falls on the determination of some systemic structural transformations and changes so that the welfare to be derived from the optimal socio-economic structure/ constitution, and from the social justice, ontological-functional established.

The practitioner being, thus, interested to a deserved and enduring welfare, with respect for the fundamental values of human dignity and rights, obtained both through social progress and change as well as through empowerment. In the current activity of the practitioner the client is encouraged to claim and acquire its legitimate and fundamental rights, and not to be at the mercy of others, or to beg help. The practitioner meets in this case, largely, the roles of advocate, enabler, negotiator, counselor and mediator.

The major issues which aim it to approach and solve are:

1. The greatest social and human problems of the society, mainly the poverty, economic and social polarization, social exclusion, discrimination, abuse, etc;

2. The structural inequalities and the oppressed/ marginalized practices and politics;

3. Promoting a determinist-holistic representation of the causes and factors that generate and maintain the social problems;

4. Promoting a systemic-societal approach to the welfare system, operating, at the philosophical level, with the structural-functionalist paradigm in problems solving;

5. The welfare is associated with the achievement of certain fundamental societal and political changes;

6. The social workers must work collectively, helping people to deal collectively with social problems, with the capitalist injustice and oppression (Mullaly, 2002).

In the last decades another orientation, in a subtle manner, gradually, seems to impose with increasing force. It's about the humanistic orientation and the logical expression, formed and enforced fairly recent and prudent in the specific literature: *Humanistic Social Work* - syntagma, theory and method that are in process of establishing and remains to be seen whether they will get to sit alongside Traditional/ Conventional Social Work and Critical/ Radical Social Work, alongside their theories and methods, and especially if it will impose, in a coherent way, in the current practice of the professionals and agencies.

The process is closely linked to the offensive of the humanistic psychology and psychotherapy, on the one hand, and microsociology and humanistic sociology, on the other hand. All in the context designed by the phenomenology, existentialism and postmodernism/ Transmodernism in the social theory and practice areas (Payne, 2011).

So, the abundance of the concepts and theories, methods and techniques from humanistic psychology and psychotherapy, from humanistic sociology and microsociology justify the observation that we can be, already, in the presence of **a *third way*** in social work, **Humanistic Social Work**, with almost certain perspective to become dominant in the future.

The explanation is found in the fact that humanistic social work incorporates concepts and methods from the two established stances, but also brings many new elements, according to the new social, human, economic, political, cultural realities and trends, and the new achievements in science and practice.

In this way, in addition, it can be stated that humanistic social work could become one of the most important doctrinal/ methodological solution for many social and human problems at the beginning of the third millennium.

The necessity of a humanistic approach in social work, with emphasis on the theories and practices of empowerment (persons and communities) and empathy, humanity and spirituality (as means of socio-human solidarity and therapeutic relationship), became evident especially after the fall of communism in Central and Eastern European countries, which collapsed several aspirations to achieving a society without inequality and oppression and with the advent of the economic crisis, which reduced many resources with whom to be helped the vulnerable people, individuals and social groups in need or difficulty, through the redistribution arrangements and social control, shocking seriously the welfare state.

The two major social, political and economic events have heavily affected the ontological and ideological foundation of the critical/ radical social work (anti-communist revolutions), and of the traditional/ conventional social work (economic crisis).

Such, has been greatly affected the project of the structural societal change, the construction of a society without oppression, social injustice, inequality, discrimination and poverty, especially through socio-political progress, radical change, even revolution, promoted by the radical/ critical/ structural social work, and of helping the vulnerable groups, individuals/ people in need, in suffering, through the welfare state and social solidarity within the capitalist society, promoted by traditional/ conventional social work.

In the light of these ideas and socio-political realities it can be stated that humanistic social work can necessarily imposes as the third force, way of social work/ welfare, fact facilitated, also, by the existence, since the establishment of social work/ welfare as current practice, more or less institutionalized/ nationalized, of the humanistic values and principles, and the presence, increasingly consistent, of the theories and methods originating in other areas of the humanistic theory and practice, mainly in humanistic psychology/ psychotherapy with sub-domains such as client-centered psychotherapy, existential psychology/ psychotherapy, gestalt psychology/ psychotherapy, strength-centered counseling, etc.

Trying a parallel with humanistic psychology, called the third way/ force in psychology (Bugental, 1964), after, or alongside psychoanalysis and behaviorist psychology, it can be identified similarities with the positioning of the humanistic social work facing to traditional social work and critical/ radical social work, placing on the same side psychoanalysis with traditional social work, and in the other side the behaviorist psycho-logy with critical/ radical social work.

Of course, the comparison and associations can seem forced, or circumstantial, but is, however, a fact, that psychoanalysis and traditional social work are important forms of onset of psychology and social assistance, both interested and focused on the body, emotions, with little interest in systemic or exterior determinism, such as, is real also the fact that the behaviorist psychology and critical/ radical social work emphasizes the role of the social system, environment, education, context in determining the problems and difficult situations of the clients, promoting, therefore, especially, methods that provide solutions from the outside of their subjectivity/ personality/ community.

4.10. Sources, Values, Purposes, Forms

Humanistic social work, as the third way in contemporary social work, is a theory and axiology that generates a reaffirmation/ restatement of the fundamental/ constitutional humanistic values of social work, incorporating, in the same time, in a (relative) new coherent and unitary theory, all what penetrated in social work in the last decades, especially from humanistic psychology and psychotherapy, but also from microsociology and humanistic sociology, from human rights philosophy/ movement, etc. These being, also, among the main its theoretical sources and foundations.

In this sense, regarding the most important **theoretical sources** of ideas and values for humanistic social work, M. Payne makes reference, as our interpretation, at three major theoretical areas, respectively philosophy (especially phenomenology and existentialism), psychology/ psychotherapy (especially the humanistic orientation) and sociology (especially the micro-sociology).

The specific theory of humanistic social work attempts to meets and organize, epistemological-methodological, the humanistic theory/ theories and methodology from the contemporary social work, in a system, providing both a unitary theoretical and methodological framework, and a forum for debate and professional or scientific innovation.

The Theories of Development and Empowerment (person and community), Empathy Theory, Attachment Theory and Happiness Theory are, in our view, among the most important support and/or specific theories of the third way/ orientation in contemporary social work and social welfare (Stefaroi, 2012, 2014).

The humanistic theoretical paradigm, which, up to a point, is identical with the social work as a whole, highlights, according to the most important orientations of humanistic thought, the following fundamental types of ideas, **values** and **concepts**:

- Promoting the concrete and complex human being, the individuality and personal happiness, its fundamental interests, feelings and values, the spiritual well-being of the person (Payne, 2011);

- Humane personality and humane relationship like the fundamental resources of practice (Stefaroi, 2012);

- Human dignity, social justice, equality, solidarity (Humanistische Akademie, 1998);

- The exploitation of the cultural and socio-human resources from the community and social context (Krill, 1978);

- Spiritual empowerment, personal/ human development and self-determination (Payne, 2011).

- Social justice, equal opportunities, solidarity, socio-human community, human relationships (Payne, 2011, p. 4).

Empowerment is, so, one of the fundamental means, aim and value of practice in humanistic social work, achieved mainly through re-humanization, re-spiritualization and re-enlightenment of the individual and community – starting from the idea that, in the most part, the social issues and situations of difficulty have as explanation a pronounced deficit of humanism, spirituality and culture in the people's personality, or in the socio-human communities.

Malcolm Payne (2011) associate the concept/ theory of humanistic social work with the concept-value of *human being*, also with the fundamental humanistic principles in practice such as fundamental human rights, personal and spiritual development, creativity, responsibility and social justice. So, a key concept and value of the humanistic social work theory and axiology it is *human being*. The professional-client interaction is, so, actually, an inter-human relationship between two or more beings, with personality and soul, and, the success of intervention is crucial determined by its nature and quality and not just by the economic resources or the used technology (Payne, 2011).

In conclusion, through imposing of the system-concept "humanistic social work" in the social work theory and literature it is marks the transition into a new phase, where the humanistic orientation enhances and enriches their actual presence, and makes it, more than an occasional association of terms, a strong and unitary theory, and a distinct theoretical and methodological paradigm/ way of social work and social welfare.

Starting from the stipulations regarding the mission and objectives of social work in the definition given by *The International Federation of Social Workers* (IFSW), whereupon:

"Social work is a practice-based profession and an academic discipline that promotes social change and development, social cohesion, and the empowerment and liberation of people. Principles of social justice, human rights, collective responsibility and respect for diversities are central to social work. Underpinned by theories of social work, social sciences, humanities and indigenous knowledge, social work engages people and structures to address life challenges and enhance wellbeing" (http://ifsw.org/)

- we may emphasize, highlights or develop the humanistic substance of the definition regarding the social work **mission and objectives**, saying that the main mission and objectives of the (humanistic) social work are to *promotes socio-human change, spiritual, cultural, and human development, socio-human cohesion, spiritual and human emancipation of people, respecting the principles of social justice, human rights, responsibility and respect for diversities, underpinned by theories of social work, social sciences, humanities and indigenous knowledge, engaging people and structures to address life challenges and enhance* *wellbeing through humane and spiritual/ cultural empowerment of the person/ client and community/ family.*

In this connection, going further, the core mission and task of humanistic social work would be to promote a compathetic attitude in the practitioner-client relationship, by creating a socio-human environment based on empathy, love and humanity, by humanizing the community, by changing the customers and communities through empowerment, personal/ community development and responsibility, starting from the person/ community's right to happiness and well-being, but also from their right to dignity and self-determination.

So, one of the most important tasks of the humanistic social work/ worker is the interventions in the personal and social crises, dramatic or at limit situations. The professionals from social work services are faced also with social and human problems caused by political or economic crises, social, natural or health disasters, blows, with great economical, psychological or medical impact. Some of these cannot be overcome because of the force of impact, damaging, irreparably, destinies, lives, careers, families, communities.

The affected people and communities experiences individual or collective dramas, impossible to describe, which the workers from social services must to intuit the human dimension, to represent them at the true intensity and meaning, to be helpful and to intervene through the humanistic social work methods, to improve the situations, relief of suffering and mitigate the effects, especially on children (Payne, 2011).

So, decrease the pain of unhappy customer, growth the spiritual well-being, personal development and gaining autonomy through empowerment, personal/ social/ moral/ spiritual development and social-human integration are other important tasks of the humanistic practitioner (Stefaroi, 2012).

In the complex and unitary methodological context the humanistic practitioner will focus especially on the spiritual, psychological and socio-human sphere of the client's personality. The goal is also the ontological harmonization of internal and external relationships within the group/ community, with effects on the development of the personality's ontological consistency of the person/ client and diminishing the risk to entry in difficult situation (Ellenhorn, 1988).

So, one of the most important task of the humanistic social worker is to enable the client, a person or community, to become capable of coping with the crisis situations and difficult situations which can appears any time. This must to promote, also, as values and objectives, the social justice, personal development of the customers, the complexity of human being, methodological flexibility, valorization of the client's creativity, development of the self and the capitalization of spiritual potential of the human personality. The humanistic social worker have also a consistent role of educator, trainer, which involves mainly giving information and developing skills to clients (Humanistische Akademie, 1998).

As is well known, in social and human sciences, the term humanist/ humanistic/ humanism was consecrated through many meanings. We hold mainly two:

1. regarding to the human condition, the idea of ancestral human unity and solidarity; the representation of person as ontological part of a human community, mutual conditioned by the human-ontogenetic interpersonal interaction - theoretical-axiological sources of the social/ human solidarity, socio-human adaptation, and concern/ care for each other;

2. regarding to the intrinsic resources and capacities of the individual, as person, of affirmation, self-actualization, self-determination, personal achievement and development; the representation of the person as me, personality, with the attribute of will and freedom, creativity, responsibility and dignity - the sources of the personal and social change and empowerment, of the individual and the community.

The first meaning is, with predilection, exploited and stated by philosophy, religion, transpersonal psychology and anthropology, while the second by humanistic and positive psychology, pedagogy, psychotherapy and humanistic sociology.

In agreement with the two established theoretical-axiological meanings also the humanistic orientation from social work generates two relatively distinct, **forms, approaches, theories** of humanistic social work, i.e. the solidarist-humanistic social work and the positive/ existential-humanistic social work.

Solidarist-humanistic social work, supported, therefore, theoretically, methodologically and axiologically by philosophy, religion, transpersonal psychology and anthropology, the solidarist-humanistic social work is closer or even identical, to some extent, with traditional social work, prioritizing the care for comfort and welfare of the helpless person, for relieving the suffering, through various forms of help, assistance, through solidarity, altruism, compassion, attachment, empathy and compathy.

Positive/ existential-humanistic social work is closer to critical social work, through the interest for changing, but not for changing the social system, the society as a whole, but through empowerment, through the exploitation and capitalization of the resources of personality and of the socio-human context with the theoretical support of the humanistic psychology, psychotherapy, pedagogy and sociology (microsociology/ humanistic sociology).

Although, strictly analytic, seems somewhat opposite, in fact, the two forms, solidarist-humanistic social work and positive-humanistic social work, are "two faces of the same coin", two sides and dimensions of the same process, subsumed to an unitary theory and practice of the humanistic social work, within the larger theoretical-methodological framework of the social work field as a whole (Stefaroi, 2012).

4.11. The Client and the Practitioner

In humanistic social work **the client** is, before any consideration of administrative, professional or scientific order, a personality, a concrete existential individuality, a soul, and not a simple (dysfunctional) element of a social entity, or a name in a file.

In this sense, because, in practice, from the humanistic social work principles and objectives perspective, between the practitioner's personality and the client's personality, especially in casework, in caring, therapy and education, is established a high psychological-ontological congruence (emotional, empathetic, humane, spiritual) the cultivation of the spiritual, humane and eudemonic-altruistic values and resources of the **practitioner**'s personality and behavior must becomes an important theoretical and methodological concern.

To this end, the specific literature, from a postmodern and transmodernposition, must promote an innovative approach on the client and the professional's qualities and conducts, with a great attention paid to the humane and psycho-spiritual qualities such as empathy and compathy, spiritual welfare and virtue, happiness and eudemonic-altruistic energy/ motivation, personal development, humane development and humanity.

Therefore, the professional's humane personality should be considered the main resource of the client's rehabilitation, of the humanistic social work practice, both when we pursue the psychological-eudaimonical objectives or the integrative, prosocial objectives.

It is, so, more than obvious the necessity of prioritization the development of the professional's psychological-ontological sphere too, the axiological-moral/ prosocial sphere, the motivational-energetical sphere, with a great attention paid to the humane soul and spiritual soul; in conclusion, to the humane personality.

Essential humane and spiritual qualities in working with the clients, such as empathy/ compathy, agreeability, tolerance, humanity, virtue, and other, are generated, largely, by the existence and manifestation of the humane personality, especially of the humane soul and spiritual soul, of course on the background and in the light of the overall personal, human and psychosocial development.

Through his humane personality, humane soul and spiritual soul, through the overall personal, human and psychosocial development, through his humane and spiritual qualities the professionals will send and stimulate the development of the humane and spiritual features at the customers too, factually sending to them positive energy, happiness, aesthetic, intellectual, spiritual, playful energy and qualities; thus contributing at their personal development, increasing the self-esteem, social consciousness, the capacity of initiative, social autonomy; will transmits empathy, humanity, agreeability, happiness and balance to the customers, will help, so, their personal/ human development, enhancing the positive perspectives of social reintegration and personal rehabilitation (Stefaroi, 2012).

Through the humane and spiritual qualities the worker's personality becomes sensitive to the sufferings and problems of the people in need, and, at the behavioral level, acquires agreeability (Hoffman, 2000). Through these qualities a worker from a residential institution for children, for example, can create a magical psychosocial and humane "universe" for satisfying the intimate, deep, emotional personal needs, can stimulate the spiritual growth and education, psychosocial and moral development of the children.

The professionals to whom the humane ego and humane soul are high developed acquire solidarist-humanistic qualities, traits such as empathy, agreeableness, tolerance etc.; the humane soul especially, having a determinant role in the formation of the humanistic, solidarist, humanitarian beliefs, convictions of the professional; also having a very important role in the orientation of the professional's character, in determining the attitudes towards themselves, towards work, people, values, society etc., towards the people in need and suffering, towards the client.

4.11 The Humanistic Social Work Methodology and Practice

The human suffering, unhappiness, personal failure, loss, dehumanization of the individual and community, emotional drama and great collective tragedies, disasters with significant human impact, personal/ community underdevelopment are among the central **problems and object of intervention** in humanistic social work practice. From here starts humanistic social work the demarche of establishing his specific objectives of practice (Stefaroi, 2012).

Operating into the sphere of social, *human* relationships, the main purpose of the services and professional's activity is that *to transform them in humane relationships, starting from the idea that the suffering, unhappiness, personal failure, loss, dehumanization of the individual and community have, largely, the main sources in the precarious social and human relationships.*

The professional's personality and its psychological-spiritual qualities represents, for this purpose, the means, the essential professional resource that can facilitate the achievement of the humanistic objectives in practice, that can facilitate the changing, through which can humanize the troubled social relationships, the dehumanized, dysfunctional micro-community, the moral, psychological damaged people, in difficulty, suffering, conflict, underdevelopment.

In this way reaching so to perform the specific mission, to determine changes not at the society level, such as the critical/radical social work, where it is the mission of the politician, nor at the body level, where it is the mission of the healthcare professional, but at the human, socio-human level, at the human relationships level, where it is its mission.

In this mission the humanistic practitioner is involved with whole its self, soul, intellect and experience, in the complex assembly of relations, connections, conflicts, attachments, inter-empathies, compathies, feelings, passions, loves, projects, dramas of the group with problems, he detect the dysfunctions, problems, under-developments, anomalies, building the diagnostic panel by an etiology and phenomenology of existential-humanistic type, focusing, therefore, on *highlighting the dysfunctions from the human relations level,* the intervention aiming, so, to convert them, by means of its knowledge, experiences, humane personality, soul, and psychological-spiritual qualities, as curative resources, in *humane relationships.*

The change for better from the human relations level, transformed into humane relations, will generate improvements, impressive qualitative changes at the micro-community level as a whole, as well at the level of each person; *the transformative process evolving in cascade, involving humanizing sub-processes at all levels, eliminating many dysfunctions, disorders, problems, sufferings; the new created environment being defined by qualifiers such as spiritual and humane welfare, efficiency, socio-humane cohesion, harmony, solidarity, mutual aid, compathy, responsible, cooperation, humanity.*

This environment will impose, ultimately, as a curative solution for many problems and difficult situations, and only to the extent that the professionals and social services manage to lead, generate it, with their activities, measures, conducts can sustain that they operates thoroughly and efficiently, and meet their specific mission, at least in the perspective of the humanistic social work theory and axiology.

Combining thus, in its own and creative way, the resources from the person level, respectively of the humane personality, with the resources from the community level, respectively of the humane relationships, taking thus elements both from traditional social work and critical/ radical social work, humanistic social work justify their attribute as the third way also and in practice.

In this sense, when they define the objectives and humanistic mission, the professionals and the social work/ welfare services operates mainly with terms and phrases such as:

- Diminishing the customer's suffering, distress and unhappy;
- Increasing the spiritual well-being (Goldstein, 1984);
- Personal and community development, and obtaining the autonomy (Payne, 2011);
- Moral development and socio-human integration, etc.

Humanistic social work practice put at the base of the services and professionals' activity, as *core value*, the client representation and approach as a *human being*, with soul, with feelings, with sufferings, with spiritual and eudaimonical needs, as personality, with ego, will, freedom and internal resources for rehabilitation and regaining the autonomy, and not just as a dysfunctional element in a social system and process. In this sense, the professional-client interaction is actually an inter-human/ humane relationship between two or more human beings, with personalities and souls, and, the success of intervention is crucial determined by its humane nature, quality and development.

Other **crucial practical values** which must stay at the basis of the services and professional's activity, would be:

- social justice (Payne, 2011);

- personal and human development of the customers:

- the complexity of the client's personality, and of the client system;

- methodological flexibility (Payne, 2011);

- evidence-based practice;

- valorization of the client's creativity, freedom and resources;

- development of the self, and the capitalization of spiritual potential;

- the priority of the client's interests, feelings and values;

- spiritual well-being and development of the client and community (Humanistische Akademie,1998);

- human development, empowerment and self-determination of the person/client and community (Stefaroi, 2012);

- equality, solidarity, compathy;

- human relationships as humane relationships;

- multiculturalism (Wing Sue, 2006);

- the importance of the professional's personality, education, humane qualities, conducts, value and principles in practice (Humanistische Akademie,1998).

Basic values of the professional in practice:

- humanism, empathy, understanding (Payne, 2011);

- frankness, accountability, discipline;
- doing good, respect for life, loyalty, cooperation, solidarity;
- courtesy, democratic spirit, kindness, concern, caring, giving, sharing;
- incorruptibility, respect of rights, non-violence;
- self-respect, happiness, contentment;
- truth, love;
- integrity, non-discrimination, honesty;
- humanistic/ altruistic motivation (Stefaroi, 2012);
- self-knowledge, concentration, meditation, self-control, temperance;
- gentleness, respect, resourcefulness, circumspection;
- forgiveness, equanimity;
- spirituality (Humanistische Akademie, 1998).

Accountability, achieving personal and social equality, flexibility in human life and professional practice, complexity in human life and professional practice, achieving caring and creativity, developing self and spirituality, developing security and resilience, developments in research are, according to Payne (2011), the most important **principles** of the humanistic social work practice.

The main role of the humanistic social work practice is to enable the clients to realize their potential within the therapeutic relationship and socio-human context, by enhancing the client's potential, to achieve the self-actualization in social environment, also to create just social conditions to promote general well-being, to promote human and social well-being by developing the human capacities, social justice, equality, freedom, and mutual responsibility through shared social experience (Payne, 2011, p. 31).

According to Payne the *accountability principle*, in humanistic social work, involves both the social worker and agency's responsibility and the client's responsibility. The client has, the first, the responsibility for his situation and his rehabilitation, but the social worker, as agent of community and humanity, has the professional accountability for applying the most optimal and scientific procedures, based on evidences, and to fulfill the mission given by these.

So, the professional has also a personal accountability, in relation of the humanitarian mission that he has, and of the specific of profession which he has chosen. Also, procedures that allow for informed consent and advanced care planning communicate respect for clients to make their own decisions upon full disclosure of information. This allows for client responsibility to express personal power or social agency.

To this end, accountability involves working together to create a social environment that is responsive to and supportive of client change. Here professional involves helping clients exercise political power when conditions are most receptive to social change. An environment most conducive to change is partially characterized by the presence of social policies that protect basic human rights (*from* Callahan, 2012, pp. 181-184).

Both principles of the humanistic social work practice, according to Payne, suggest an almost limitless human and professional opening to a wide variety possibilities of manifestation of the customer and to the multiple therapeutic options. The *flexibility principles* guides especially the current practitioner activity; it facilitates a flexible assistential/ therapeutic relationship that consists of an improvisation that occurs between the client and professional, and is articulated through the convention of therapeutic/ assistential rapport.

The *complexity principle* concerns the way of representation to the client, the social context and the difficult situation, especially in the way of approach and assessment activity. Payne considers that the complexity principle involves a complex and multidimensional representation of the client, of the situations of difficulty and therapeutic contexts in which operate the professional. Reactions to change may not be accurately predicted given the variety of factors involved in a system. So, the author warns against oversimplification of relational patterns that may come with problem solving, and encourages fuller consideration of a variety of perspectives to better respond to the multifaceted nature of client concerns (*from* Callahan, 2012, pp. 181-184).

For Payne, in humanistic social work practice, *the spirituality principle* is one of the most important. After the author of the book "Humanistic Social Work. Core Principles in Practice" spirituality is one of unlimited resources that are available to both at the client and the professional and involves the process of making meaning out of life events. Through spirituality the intervention process can help the clients to establish a sense of congruence with self and the world, with culture, wholeness in life and happiness (Payne, 2011).

What would particularizes a **code of ethics** of the humanist social work practice in report to critical and/ or radical social work for example, which emphasizes the importance of the systems and structures generators of problems, inequality, suffering, social injustice, is the emphasis put, in the work of the services and professionals, on the exploitation of the resources of the personalities and socio-human contexts involved in the processes of assessment and intervention.

This aspect involves a huge responsibility of the services and professionals which one can not invoke the system and structures for the failure of activity, and require from them very much engagement, responsibility, ethics, knowledge, skills, and professional relationships marked themselves of more humanism.

In humanistic social work "system" every professional has an active role in the promotion, development and advancement of all integrated social policies aimed at fostering social and civic advancement, emancipation and responsibility within the community, and in any programs designed to improve the quality of life.

Also, the professional must deal with his colleagues, and any other professionals, with whom he is working, in a manner that is honest, polite, loyal and in a spirit of collaboration.

In humanistic social work practice the professional's work, conduct and decision is based on scientific elements of the profession at all levels and in all their various forms, along with the ethical and moral ideals it embodies. He must act in a committed manner and under professional supervision and research.

Despite the appearances, the humanistic social work praxeology grant great importance to the scientific method, to research and **the evidence-based practice**.

It uses the evidence-based practices and methods to understand and address, scientifically and experimentally, the human relationships and behavior, human growth, the social issues, the situations of difficulty of the clients (Roberts, Yeager, 2006).

The evidence-based practices and methods, in humanistic social work practice, propose, in the specific activity of evaluation, intervention and change, in casework, caring and therapy, etc., the focusing on the complex, phenomenological reality of the client by scientific knowledge, experimental research and methodical embedding of the previous clinical experiences.

So, in humanistic social work practice the practitioners can/ must embody flexible, contextual, but also knowledge-based responses to the complexities of the human personality and community, to the complexity of the situations of difficulty of the clients (Payne, 2011).

In this sense, the evidence-based practices involves, in the specific activity of the practitioner, of assessment and intervention, the focusing, both contextual/ existential and scientific, on the complex, phenomenological reality of the client (Rubin, Babbi, (2012).

The construction of the evaluative picture of system client starts, yet, with what is identified as existing, real, verifiable and sensitive (Payne, 2011: 76). Further, the practitioner's work is based on the evidence of researches and studies's conclusions on that type of case it works. This having the task to realize "modelations" of the identified difficult situations in report of the research's findings, without abdicating, but, the fundamental values and principles of the humanistic social work related to the immense complexity of the socio-human phenomena and of the situations of difficulty in which are involved the clients (O'Hare, 2005).

Appreciative Methods promote, as objective, but also as the main strategy, the solving of social/ human problems through the appreciation, knowledge and increasing the optimistic, positive worker and client's expectations related to the client's evolution and the results of the intervention/ support activity (Bellinger, Elliott, 2011).

Operates with the conventional instruments of social work, like social inquiry, supervision, intervention project and case management, but are still resized by categories of the optimistic methods, and takes crucial paradigms from positive psychology, cognitive psychology or psychotherapy. The appreciative social inquiry respects some principles like the constructionist principle, of simultaneity, poetic principle, positive principle or of anticipation.

Balance Method Is a humanistic method both of evaluation and intervention/ support/ care (Mc Call, 2001). In the humanistic social work practice it can operate with the following onto-balances:

- the balance of socio-affective onto-systems;

- the balance of socio-cognitive onto-systems;

- the balance of relationships and role-status onto-systems;

- the balance of attitudinal, cultural and spiritual onto-systems, etc. (Stefaroi, 2012).

Payne (2011) consider **caring** more important than **helping**. But he states that it is about of a holistic and humanistic caring, that includes the personality and spirituality, not only the physical and emotional spheres.

"Humanistic social work focuses more than many models of social work practice on holistic caring processes rather than helping for two reasons. One is that many social work and similar services are involved in helping people with long-term-care needs; children whose parents cannot care for them; people with mental illnesses, intellectual, and physical disabilities; and older people. Therefore, social work requires more than a quick problem-solving intervention or social change and then standing aside; it requires developing the client's personal capacities to resolve difficulties and live an improved quality of life over a long-term involvement. Second, social work aims at psychological efficacy, as humanistic psychotherapies envisage, but it also involves a focus on empowering the social agency of social networks in the client's environment." (Payne, 2011, p. 139).

To this end, in our opinion, it is essential that everyone who works, for example, in residential/ care institutions to meet a minimum conditions of human, educational, vocational, psychological or moral order. The organizations where they work must to be themselves a source of stability, efficiency and humanism for the customers (Stefaroi, 2007).

That because the empathetic ability, the emotional wellbeing, happiness, the personal development, altruism, agreeability, intelligence, culture, idealism, visionary orient the workers through the achievement of the humane/ humanistic goals of the care institution. The positive effects are felt over time particularly by shifting the focus from the care of body to the care of spirit and personality.

Chapter 5

The Humanistic Approach and Method in Pedagogy and Education

Content

The
Humanistic Approach
in
Psychology & Psychotherapy,
Sociology & Social Work,
Pedagogy & Education,
Management and Art:

Personal Development
and
Community Development

5.1. Introductory Aspects

In great measure, the humanistic paradigm of pedagogy and education is a replica of the humanistic paradigm of psychology and psychotherapy, the humanistic psychological theory and methodology succeeded, gradually, to make place in the pedagogy's literature and educational practice through values, objectives and terms such as *human and personal development, happiness, self-determination, person/child-centered education, positive education* etc., also to determine even a shift of emphasis to humanistic and positive values and goals of the education as institution.

Personality, as core category, values, objective and resource in humanistic pedagogy and education is addressed in this chapter of the book by the two cardinal guidelines of the humanistic theory/ approach, respectively *existential-positive* and *ontological-spiritual/humane*, speaking, therefore, in the humanistic-ontological perspective of *spiritual/ humane personality,* and, in existential-positive perspective of *strong* and *developed personality.* The education, personal development, professional and social formation and development, core objectives in humanistic education, being obtained by the mobilization, development and control of these resources in the educational process.

Essentially, the humanistic paradigm of education as process and activity brings in the forefront concepts and ideas such as child/student-centered approach, self-determination, self-actualization, the power/force of the ego, personality, consciousness, strength-based education/teaching, spirituality, empowerment, personal development, personal accomplishment, holistic assessment and teaching, optimism, creativity, happiness, the child's uniqueness, focus on the particular aspects of its human coexistence, tolerance, love, etc.

From a humanistic-positive position it is highlighted the importance in the educational process/ activity of some issues and resources as the strengths, the virtues, the talents of the child/ student, its positive experiences of learning, the positive relationships, happiness, the states of pleasure or flow, the positive emotions, the orientation of the learning to future, the positive expectations, appreciations, etc.

Essentially, the humanistic and positive pedagogies promote especially the formation, in the educational process, of the personality, of the person as a whole, as person in socio-human context, putting the objectives which aim the intellectual formation in second plan, yet without disregarding them. That is the reason way in process are used operational objectives as personality formation, personality development, personality empowerment, self-realization, psychological-personal development and empowerment, the humanization and spiritualization of the child/ student.

The existential directions/ modalities/ approaches focuses on the inner capacity of self-determination and formation of the child's personality, based on free will and self-realization, while the spiritual (humane, ontological, etc.) approaches focus on the formation, through education, of the child/ student as spiritual and humane personality.

In general, the humanistic approach in pedagogy and education prioritizes the role of some formative factors such as the human/humane quality of the adults' personalities, of the social, interpersonal, relationships, crucial role having in this sense the human quality of the learning community. Here we consider mainly the family and the school class, but also the communities of friends, neighbors, relatives etc. Both the family and the school class must be represented more than mere social groups, but especially like human/humane, spiritual, cultural, compathetic communities, that have essential contributions especially in the formation of social personality, core objective in humanistic education.

The humanistic perspective on the parent/teacher operates with a concept of professional personality of humane-spiritual type, which combines, dialectically, the humane and spiritual dimension with the one pragmatic. Empathy, spiritual welfare, humane and personal development and spiritual sensibility are crucial, indispensable traits of the teacher in humanistic pedagogy. These crucial interpersonal qualities and resources, involved in the educational process, have, mainly, as psychological-ontological source, its humane and spiritual personality, but also its strong personality.

The teacher/adult's personality is important especially in the educational objectives that involve the personal and human empowerment/development/formation. The theories of personality (development) describe and approach the child/student as *human being* situated in *process* of psychological, human, emotional and social development, where the adults' personalities have great contributions.

In this sense, crucial resources of education promoted by the humanistic pedagogy are empathy, happiness and love (attachment), being used as formative instruments, ways by the educators in achieving objectives as psychological-human and social-personal development, the educator-child educational relationship being in fact a framework for transfer humanity and spirituality, a subtle lane that the educator uses, intentionally and professionally, to achieve the assumed educational goals.

5.2. Humanistic Pedagogy and Education

As it was established, consecrated, affirmed, in theory and practice, **humanistic pedagogy,** as science, proposes and promotes, in essence, the displacement of emphasis, in the educational process, from the teacher and method on the child/ student, and the exploitation of its psychological and spiritual resources of learning, growing, developing, creativity and self-affirmation (Hall and Hall, 1988; Vico, 1993).

In this sense, humanistic pedagogy promotes mainly the representation of the child/ student as *ego* and *personality*, the power of its consciousness and will, its freedom and responsibility to self-determination, the ontogenetical and scholar evolution/ development in accordance with its bio-psycho-social characteristics and choices (R. Steiner, 1996).

From the humanistic pedagogy's position, every healthy child has the capacity to self-determination, has the capacity to use its potential in human, social and spiritual terms; all depends of its internal activism and of the willingness for change or self-fulfillment.

These are also some of the main resources of the humanistic pedagogy and its applications in education and teaching, which bring, therefore, in the forefront concepts and ideas such as:

> ➢ child/ student-centered approach,
>
> ➢ self-determination, self-actualization,
>
> ➢ the power/ force of the ego, personality, and consciousness,
>
> ➢ strength-based education/ teaching,
>
> ➢ spirituality,
>
> ➢ empowerment,
>
> ➢ personal development,
>
> ➢ personal accomplishment,

- ➤ holistic assessment and education,

- ➤ optimism, creativity, happiness,

- ➤ the individual/ child uniqueness,

- ➤ focus on the particular aspects of its human existence, tolerance, love, etc. (R. Steiner, 1996; Hall and Hall, 1988; Vico, 1993; M. Montessori, 1968).

According to Rogers, who dedicated a great attention to humanistic pedagogy and education, the child/ student's need to achieving personal fulfillment is a crucial way for it psychological and scholar development.

Regarding the **humanistic education,** as process, activity and action, it involves the education as were consecrated these practically and not declarative, but is not limited to these, it exceeds, completes and fulfills through the interest and focus on the child/ student and the educational process as a whole, through the interest and focusing on the ontological-spiritual aspects of the educational process, both in family as well in the school, proposing, therefore, educational objectives relating to the condition as personality of the child/ student, focusing both on the formation of the interior psychological-ontological structures, as well as on the involvement, in the comprehensive educational process, to the interpersonal, social, cultural resorts which determines, ontogenetically, structurally, functionally and existentially, the formation of the student/ child as a person; on the one hand, developed personally, humanly and spiritually, and, on the other hand, ego-personally fulfilled and socio-humanely integrated (R. Steiner, 1972; M. Montessori, 1968).

5.3. Positive Pedagogy and Education

Positive Pedagogy is a relatively new field of academic study, being considered either an autonomous science, either a part of the humanistic pedagogy, either an extension of the humanistic psychology. Probably all the affirmations are valid.

This pedagogical discipline investigates and proposes the formation end development of specific skills that assist the child/ student to strengthen their relationships, build positive emotions, enhance personal resilience, promote mindfulness and encourage a healthy lifestyle (Seligman & Fowler, 2011).

Essentially, this kind of pedagogy highlights the importance in the educational process/ activity of some issues and resources as the:

- strengths, virtues, talents;

- positive experiences of learning;

- positive relationships and communities;

- happiness, states of pleasure or flow;

- positive emotions;

- orientation of the learning to the future;

- positive expectations, appreciations;

- empathy (M. Montessori, 1968; Seligman & Fowler, 2011).

Positive Education, as process, activity and action, is focuses especially on flourishing, formation and development of the child/ student through learning on multiple levels that include the biological, personal, relational, institutional, cultural, and global dimensions of life.

On of the most important aim of positive education in the psychological-personal development through the use of the psycho-eudaimonical, psycho-volitional and adaptive resources, developing, therefore, its existential, hedonic and adaptive dimension, the happiness, the freedom, responsibility and the will, the formation of traits and qualities such as general psychological wellbeing, activism, self-determination, freedom-accountability, optimism, energy, free will, self-realization, hope, active consciousness, personal development, social adaptability, assertiveness, resilience, happiness, etc. (Seligman & Fowler, 2011; Vico, 1993)

Therefore, essentially, positive pedagogy as theory and positive education as practice bring together the science of positive psychology with the best practices in teaching to encourage and support the child to psychologically flourish and personal developing, as a combination of feeling good and doing good.

5.4. Core Objectives

Humanistic and positive pedagogies promote especially the formation, in the educational process, of the personality, of the person as a whole, putting the objectives which aim the intellectual formation in second plan, yet without disregarding them.

That is the reason way in process are used terms, ideas, values as:

- personality formation;
- personality development;
- personality empowerment;
- self-actualization;
- child/ student's intern potential;
- personality transfer and empathy;
- psychological-personal development and empowerment;
- child/ student-centered-intervention;
- existential education;
- gestalt pedagogy;
- transpersonal pedagogy;
- spiritual education
- the humanization of the child/ student;

- the spiritualization of the child/ student, etc. (R. Steiner, 1972; M. Montessori, 1968; Seligman & Fowler, 2011).

Essentially, in humanistic pedagogy are dominant two great directions/ modalities/ approaches regarding the educational goals:

- existential (positive, phenomenological, etc.), and;
- spiritual (humane, ontological, etc.).

The existential directions/ modalities/ approaches focuses on the inner capacity of self-determination and formation of the child's personality, based on free will and self-realization.

The spiritual (humane, ontological, etc.) approaches focus on the formation, through education, of the child/ student as spiritual and humane personality.

In the first case the objectives aim principally the personal development, highlighted of traits as:

- Personal and social autonomy;
- Interpersonal development;
- Mature personality, adaptability;
- Personal and social efficiency (Rogers, 1977, 1980);
- Socio-emotional development, control of emotions, emotional intelligence;
- Realism and balance;
- Powerful will, resistance to failure and frustrations;
- Hope, orientation to future. positive attitude, optimism, active thinking (Seligman, 2002);
- High degree of awareness, self-knowledge, self-esteem (Maslow, 2011);
- Professional development;
- Activism, self-determination;

- Optimism, energy, free will;

- Active consciousness;

- Social adaptability, assertiveness, resilience,

- Happiness, etc. (Seligman & Fowler, 2011; Vico, 1993).

Regarding the spiritual (humane, ontological) formation of the child/ student, the objectives, in the educational process, aim principally the spiritual and humane development, the formation of a structure of personality dominated of traits as:

- Spirituality;

- Humanity;

- Empathy;

- Altruism;

- Generosity;

- Kindness;

- Morality;

- Virtue;

- Sociality;

- Love, attachment;

- Socio-human efficiency and adaptability, etc. (R. Steiner, 1972; M. Montessori, 1968).

Through the fulfillment of the spiritual and humane objectives of education the child/ student's personality can be described both as personality developed at a higher level, the most high, the most close to the condition of human being as autonomous cultural, rational, spiritual existence, with its characteristic attributes - morality, virtue, sociality, spirituality, personal development, adaptability and socio-human efficiency, and as personality structured through the self, ego, conscience, character, motivation, skills, etc. so that determines conducts oriented towards the wellbeing of the generalized other, towards the common good, humanity, and dominant traits such as empathy, altruism, generosity, kindness, etc. (R. Steiner, 1972; M. Montessori, 1968; Seligman & Fowler, 2011).

5.5. The Learning Community

In humanistic and positive pedagogy the optimal learning community is the one that assures, facilitates, stimulates, leads both to the formation of a strong personality, evidenced by features such as high capacity for self-determination, optimism, energy, free will, active consciousness, social adaptability, assertiveness, resilience, happiness, personal and social autonomy, interpersonal development, mature personality, adaptability, personal and social efficiency, socio-emotional development, control of emotions, emotional intelligence, realism and balance, powerful will, resistance to failure and frustrations, hope, orientation to future. positive attitude, optimism, active thinking, high degree of awareness, self-knowledge, self-esteem, professional development, activism, etc., as well as to the formation of the human and spiritual sphere, dimension of the child/ student's personality, characterized by qualities such as spirituality, virtue, altruism, generosity, kindness, morality, sociality, love, attachment, socio-human efficiency and adaptability, humanity/ humanness, empathy, etc.

Thus, the humanistic approach in pedagogy and education prioritizes the role of some factors such as the human quality of the adults' personalities, of the social, interpersonal, relationships, but crucial role has the human quality of the learning community. Here we consider mainly the family and the school class, but also the communities of friends, neighbors, relatives etc.

Both the family and the school class must be represented, in humanistic perspective, more than mere social groups, but especially like human, spiritual, cultural, empathetic communities, that have essential contributions especially in the formation of personality, the main objective in the humanistic education (M. Montessori, 1968).

Between the learning community and the individuals which it constitutes it is established a ontological-socio-human balance, an existential and functional optimum, in which is satisfied, in principle, in a harmonious and non-confrontational way, both the personal and the collective necessities.

But this learning community can also have a negative influences, may be an area of non-value, of conflict, hostility or social exclusion, or can have a coherent organization and functioning but founded on non-value, on antisocial attitudes, or may be poorly organized, dysfunctional, immature. In both cases, the members are exposed to personal, humane, spiritual and intellectual under-development. (R. Steiner, 1972).

The optimal educational conditions, learning community for the construction of a strong, developed, equilibrate and humane personality of the child/ studenf, both in the school class and family, but also in the communities of friends, neighbors, relatives, are the ones opposites, characterized bg qualities as positive, functional relationships, social/ human solidarity, unity, communication, cooperation, inter-empathy, humanity, altruism, responsibility. Essential being the quality of the social relationships from the learning community represented as *humane* relationships in the humanistic pedagogy.

5.5. The Student and the Educator

The epistemological foundation in the representation of **the child/ student**, from the humanistic pedagogy's perspective, is, in fact, its educational and projective-teleological representation as personality, ego, character, creative and spiritual being. Therefore, it is brings in the forefront of the educational strategies and processes, of the educational objectives, its *human, spiritual, personal and social formation and development*(Seligman & Fowler, 2011; Vico, 1993).

In the process of representation it is indicated to be involved also the system of the socio-humane relationships, the humane community.

Through the humane ego, humane conscience, and humane character the child/ student is formed, educates and exists as part of a humane community (network) of attachments, values, persons, humane relationships, and, in conclusion, its personality formation and development are conditioned by the personal-humane and compathetical-cultural quality of this community.

In relation to the two (humanistic) paradigms, perspectives of representation and approach to personality, one can speak of two types of values and resources of the child/ student's personality in the humanistic educational practice:

> of his *humane and spiritual personality,*

> and of his *strong, developed personality.*

The first is related to the term *humane and spiritual development/ resources* of the child/ student's personality, and the second to the term *personal-psychological development/ resources* of the child/ student's personality.

The syntagma child/ student's *humane and spiritual personality* refers mainly to the psychological-humane and spiritual content/ nature of the child/ student's personality, also to the humanistic orientation, quality, the overall humane and spiritual valence, dimension of the client's global personality.

Too, the issue relating the **parent/ teacher's personality** is of great importance, that's why it requires a comprehensive approach.

The model of representation is, therefore, opposed to the didactic-intellectualist model. The humanistic-ontological perspective on the parent/ teacher operates with a concept, of professional personality, of humane-spiritual type, which combines, dialectically, the humane and spiritual dimension with the one pragmatic (Vico, 1993).

That's why, also in the process of teacher education, is put accent on an applied spiritual-humanistic curriculum; the aim is that of training and cultivation of the complex professional humane personality, the ability to empathize with the student.

Empathy and compathy, spiritual welfare, humane development and spiritual sensibility are crucial, indispensable traits of the teacher in humanistic-ontological pedagogy. These crucial interpersonal qualities and resources, involved in the educational process, have, mainly, as psychological-ontological source, the humane and spiritual personality, but also its strong personality.

5.6. The (Humanistic) Educational Process

The *Humanistic* education process brings in the forefront of evaluation and educational action concepts and ideas such as:

- holistic assessment and education;
- optimism;
- creativity;
- happiness;
- the child/ student's uniqueness;
- focus on the particular aspects of its socio-human existence;
- tolerance, love, etc.
- child/student-centered approach (Rogers, 1951;
- self-determination, self-actualization;
- the power/ force of the ego, personality, and consciousness;
- strength-based education/ teaching;
- spirituality;

- empowerment;
- psychological-personal development;
- socio-human and professional accomplishment, etc. (Rogers, 1951; R. Steiner, 1972; M. Montessori, 1968; Seligman & Fowler, 2011).

The humanistic education has, inter alia, the task, to operate/ determine those compathetical, humane improvements at the level of inter-personal relationship, group, organization, family, couple, etc. that would lead, through the humanising force that exercise the socio-human/ humane relationships and the humanistic group upon the child, to beneficial improvements in its psychological and social development/ formation.

In this sense, the humanistic education/ teaching uses the human personality as core resources and values with priority in the objectives regarding the personal-psychological development and formation, where the educator, with his humane and developed global personality and behavior, succeeds to have a greater efficiency, both in the objectives involving the psychological welfare and happiness of the child, as well as in those pursuing his formation and development.

The educational process starts with the demarche of evaluation through the representation of the child as personality. That is why it is necessary the settlement, in the front-plan of the evaluative panel, of the dysfunctional elements and deviations from a so-called normality in the psychological-personal, humane and spiritual development/ wellbeing of the child/ student, evaluated in the context of some systems of human/ social relationships more or less humane/ pro-humane or developed.

In his educational activity, through his humane/ strong personality and behavior, the educator can contributes crucially to the achievement of the humanistic established objectives, mostly those related to the psychological-emotional developed of the child, those concerning the empowerment, autonomization, the social, socio-humane integration and adaptation in the community where the child lives.

From the humanistic methodology and praxeology perspective the efficiency of the educational process is high especially when it is considered the direct psychological relationship between the educator and the child. Especially through the empathetic capacity and resources of his personality the educator acquires access to the child's personality and psychological experience, and, also, acquires an effective method/ way of psychological/ humane/ spiritual development/ empowerment.

5.8. Child/ Student-Centered Education/ Teaching

The core idea of the child/ student-centered education/ teaching is that, in the educational process must to take the child's personality, desires, feelings, attitudes, beliefs, aspirations seriously, because these can be the basis for an authentic and durable education, development, formation, by finding his inner authentic resources, in his personality and concrete (circumstantial) socio-human/ educational relationships.

Essentially, this kind of education and teaching is characterized by:

- the educator experiences an empathic understanding of the child/ student's internal sentiments, desires, aspiration, ideas etc.;

- the educator must manifest increased trust in the child/ student potential and in its capacity to grow and develop with its own resources, the role of the educator being principally to guide it;

- the educational relationship must be a relationship in which each person's perception of the other is very important;

- into the framework of the educational relationship must to exist an empathetical/ compathetical congruence (emotional, cognitive etc. between the child/ student and therapist;

- the educator must accept the child/ student unconditionally, without judgment, disapproval or approval;

- the educator helps the child/ student to believe that the therapist has an unconditional love for them;

- the educator must involve in the educational relationship his own experiences to facilitate the development, emancipation, empowerment of the child/ student. (C. Rogers, 1951, R. Steiner, 1972; M. Montessori, 1968; Seligman & Fowler, 2011).

From an existential-spiritual perspective the child/ student-centered education/ teaching seeks, inter alia, as evaluation, to research/ identification the existential-spiritual and existential-humane potentialities, while, in intervention, it aims to achieve the internal-ontological spiritual rebalancing/ empowerment through spiritual growth and emancipation/ development. From a gestaltist perspective the child/ student-centered education/ teaching involves principally its representation and approach as a whole, existing and learning "here and now".

5.9. Education through Psychological-Personal, Spiritual and Human Development

Among the most important schools that promote and apply this type of humanistic and positive education should be mentioned Waldorf, Montessori, Reggio Emilia, and Neo-humanist schools.

The theories of personality (development) and (human) being in the humanistic education and teaching describe and approach of the child/ student as human being situated in process of psychological, human, emotional and social development, with his personality, desires, sentiments, knowledge as core resource for growing.

The psychological-personal, human, emotional and social development is, so, one of the most important key tool of formation as person, personality, as accomplished human being and well integrated in society when will be a mature and autonomous person (Vico, 1993).

In this sense, one of the most important way of intervention in the process of emancipation, empowerment and development of the child/ student is through *spiritualization* and *humanization*, through spiritual and human/ humane development. Even if is a very complex and difficult endeavor the humanization and spiritualization of the child is described by the theoreticians of the humanistic-spiritual pedagogy as miraculous solutions for the education in perspective of formation of a complex, profound and creative personality.

The educational process begins with what a personological-humanistic-spiritual evaluation. The epistemological foundation of the evaluation in humanistic-spiritual perspective it is, actually, the representation of the child as complex and profound personality, spiritual being.

In the spiritual-humanistic education the practitioner, through his spiritual personality and behavior, contributes crucially at the achievement of the humanistic established objectives, mostly those relating to the spiritual wellbeing of the child, but also at those concerning the empowerment, autonomization, the social, socio-humane integration and adaptation in the community where the student lives.

Through spirituality and creativity, the humanistic educator works at the construction of a new (spiritual) *modus vivendi*, of some new behaviors of the student, with humanistic-spiritual tools and methods (R. Steiner, 1972; M. Montessori, 1968).

So, with methods and behaviors of humanistic-spiritual type, the educator performs changes and re-modelings of the current spiritual, social, cultural and psychosocial situation of the child, changes and improvements in the concrete situations of depersonalization and dehumanization, in the individual and collective situations of spiritual-existential impasse, spiritual-existential crisis.

Regarding the importance of spirituality and virtue, as qualities of the educator's personality in activity effectiveness and achieving the objectives, this is given by the fact that the relationship with the child is not objectual but "spiritual", and very complex, and therefore the dominant resources involved must be also of this nature (Seligman & Fowler, 2011).

5.9. Education through Empathy, Happiness, Love and Attachment

Other sources and methods of education promoted by the humanistic pedagogy are empathy, happiness and love (attachment).

Empathy is a formative instrument used by the educators in achieving objectives as psychological-human and personal education/ development. The educator-child proactive empathetic relationship is in fact a framework for transfer, a subtle lane that the educator uses, intentionally and professionally, to achieve the assumed educational goals (C. Rogers, 1951, R. Steiner, 1972).

Crucial it is the goal regarding the humanly growing and development of the child through the development of the empathetic spheres of his personality and behavior.

Also, another role of the educator is to use or create the optimal socio-human environment for the human grow and development of the child/ student in the educational process.

Regarding the relevance and usefulness of **happiness** as important resource and method in humanistic education the aspect is revealed by ideas, facts, aspects as:

- Happiness is a source of personal development, for formation of a strong and balanced personality, social/ professional efficiency and factor for the acquisition of the autonomous social reintegration capacity;

- The student is not only a simple consumer of educational services, it is also a cultural, spiritual, aesthetic, playful being - this has therefore and emotional, cultural, spiritual, aesthetic, playful needs and resources, which, for a full valorization, must be unconditionally satisfied (Stefaroi, 2009b).

- Every person, regardless of age, sex, nationality, race, social status, profession is entitled to a dignified life, to happiness, to personal fulfillment;

- The essential indicator of the human life quality is the internal satisfaction, subjective felt, the happiness and complacency of the person (M. Montessori, 1968; Seligman & Fowler, 2011).

Regard the role of **love and attachment** as resource and method in humanistic education the humanistic theoreticians bring in attention, inter alia, the stipulations of the attachment theory that highlights the importance of affection and attachment relationships in the social/ interpersonal relationships and coexistence, especially regarding the role of *child-parent attachment*, but also of the relationships of attachment between the student and the educator in the formation of a balanced and adaptive personality of the child (Bowlby, 1999), stimulating, improving the process of learning, the formation and maturation in all the personality and behavior's areas - cognitive, emotional, social, moral, personal development, professionalization, etc. (Vico, 1993; R. Steiner, 1972).

Therefore, essentially, in theory and practice, humanistic pedagogy proposes and promotes, inter alia, the displacement of emphasis, in the educational process, from the intellectual resources, from the memory and memorization, and cognitive and intellectual development (as core objective and aim), to resources as empathy, happiness and love (attachment), and the **personal development** – as core objective and aim.

Chapter 6

The Humanistic Approach
and Method in Management and Art

Content

The
Humanistic Approach
in
Psychology & Psychotherapy,
Sociology & Social Work,
Pedagogy & Education,
Management and Art:

Personal Development
and
Community Development

6.1. Introductory Aspects

Like sociology and psychology the managerial science and practice has experienced in the second half of the twentieth century radical changes, in a large extent determined by the offensive the humanistic theory and method in all the areas of the social sciences and practices. In the context of the offensive of the humanistic sociology and psychology, the humanistic theory and methodology have manifested gradually also in management, instituting the humanistic management, but also in other domains linked theoretically to sociology, including in art and aesthetics, instituting also humanistic aesthetics.

Essentially, the **humanistic approach to management** is guided by ideas, principles, values and objectives as: the manager must manifest increased trust in the employee's potential and creativity, the employee as being, subject, self, ego matter and prevail in the relationships with the organization as a whole and with the economical goals, the manager experiences an empathetic understanding of the employee's personality and personal/ social situation/ problems, the organizational/ professional relationship must be a relationship in which each person's perception of the other is very important, the employee must be involved in the organizational processes with all his psychological-personal and organizational/ professional experiences, the manager must to contribute to the solving of the employee's personal (psychological, familial, social) problems, challenges, the manager induces a sense of freedom and mutual responsibility in organization, etc.

In **art** the **humanistic approach** is focused on ideas, aspects and goals as: the humanistic/ humane source and explanation of the artist's talent and personality, the humanistic concept of artistic personality, the humane and spiritual structure of the artistic personality, the humanistic representation and definition of the character (personage), the socio-human/ humane relationships between the characters, but also between the artists, the compathtetic community of characters, artists, etc., the humanistic screenplay and directing, the humanistic spectacle, the humanistic mission of the artistic act, etc.

6.2. Humanistic Management

Humanistic Management, as science, is an important theoretical source and methodological resource in leading the small and medium organizations, in all areas, but with predilection those from the socio-human domains.

Among the most important questions, concerns of humanistic management are:

- what attachment relationships are established between employees and between employees and leaders in the organizational relationships/ partnership, of kinship, friendship, enmity, interest, collegiality, power relationships, etc.;

- how employees adjust, interactively, their behaviors and symbolizes, mutually, the organizational existence (values, customs, rituals, behaviors);

- how employees and organizations solve humanly the professional and personal problems;

- how the persons and the organizations are adapted to the changes or react to organizational crisis or major social/ personal events. (P.L. Berger, 1963; F. Znaniecki, 1969).

From the perspective of humanistic management's principles, the employee as being, subject, self matter and prevail in the relationships with the organization as a whole and with the economical goals, the employee being not a simple element, or a tool, means for organization to achieve its objectives, but, conversely, the organization is the social frame where the employee expresses its skills and is fulfilled personally and socially.

Humanistic management, as scientific discipline focuses, especially, on the personal-subjective, socio-human processes from organization, on the interpersonal relationships and phenomena, on the cognitive and emotional, socio-human, psychological-subjective, inter-personal, inter-human, inter-psychological processes, on the concrete organizational relationships and interpersonal phenomena and processes of influence, persuasion, knowledge (organizational perception and representation), cooperation and conflict, attachment and love, but also on aspects as the organizational conformity, compliance, obedience, the interpersonal organizational attractions, etc.

Essentially, therefore, the central idea of the humanistic management theory is that the managerial act operates with humans and not with mere workers or officials (von Kimakowitz, Spitzeck, Pirson, Dierksmeier, Amann, 2011).

As well, the humanistic management theory highlights the aspect that the organization is a complex interaction between the humans' personalities that compose it and not only a mere economical interaction, of formal-institutional type, between simple organizational elements, individuals, professionals, instituting a human-compathetical organizational community.

The organizational-humane community being both a source of organizational functionality and efficiency, and also a source of personal fulfillment and happiness for the employees.

In this regard, the humanistic orientation to the managerial act and process emphasizes the aspect that the manager leads, organizes, coordinates humans with personalities and needs and not only with skills, competencies, professional and organizational skills.

6.3. Humane Organization and Strong Organization

In relation to the two main (humanistic) paradigms, perspectives of representation and approach, one can speak of two types or dimensions of the organization:

> *Humane Organization*, and

➤ *Strong Organization.*

The category/ term, syntagm **Humane Organization** brings into focus issues, features such as:

- socio-human, inter-personal organizational functionality, organizational-human integration/ cohesion;

- people-centered organization and functioning;

- dominance of the inter-personal relationships of attachment, love, respect, etc.;

- dominance of the practices and customs of mutual help into the organization;

- organizational-human/ social solidarity;

- harmony, unity, inter-personal congruency, etc. ((P.L. Berger, 1963; F. Znaniecki; von Kimakowitz, Spitzeck, Pirson, Dierksmeier, Amann, 2011).

The humane organization operates, through the humane-organizational culture, as a system of symbols or values that are rooted. in great measure, in the individual's personality or activism. These symbols and values are imposed as links and unity resorts between the parties. Their existence and operation give the sense of organizational belonging, familiar, known, give comfort, safety and happiness into the organizational framework.

Between the humane organization and the individuals is established a humane-ontological balance, an existential and functional optimum where is satisfied, existentially, in a harmonious and non-confrontational way, both the personal and the organizational/ managerial necessities/ requirements.

The syntagm, term **Strong Organization,** incorporates in great measure the term humane organization but refers especially to a set of *organizational features* such as powerful institutions, orientation to the future, planification, collaboration, good management, high functionality, strong organizational culture, strong economy, high resistance to crisis and challenges, inter-communities development, etc.

6.4. Organizational Development

From the humanistic management theory's perspective the level of organizational development are closely determined by the global level of development of the global organization, of the organization as a social/ institutional entity existing in a comprehensive, larger social/ organizational/ societal context, but especially through its humane and cultural dimensions, valences, spheres, reveled of features such as:

- High cultural development;

- High socio-human autonomy;

- High interpersonal, social development;

- High socio-human functionality;

- High inter-personal, socio-human organizational integration/ cohesion;

- People-centered organization and functioning;

- The dominance of the inter-personal relationships of attachment, love, respect, etc.;

- The dominance of the practices and customs of mutual help into the organization;

- High organizational-human/ social solidarity;

- High harmony, unity, inter-personal congruency, etc.

- Social and economical efficiency;

- High control of the processes and activities;

- High resilience;

- Dominant orientation to future. optimism, etc. (F. Znaniecki, 1969; von Kimakowitz, Spitzeck, Pirson, Dierksmeier, Amann, 2011).

In humanistic perspective the organizational efficiency is gauged through highlighting the importance of the humane and cultural resources and results as well. The great inclusive, cohesive and developed organizations incorporate, in a sublime manner, both the features of the strong organization but also of the humane organizations.

6.5. The Humanist Manager

The core idea of a humanistic approach to manager is that the manager that dispose of the qualities, capacities, and of the levers of control of the organizational-human phenomena and processes disposes of access not only to the aptitudinal resources of the subordinates but also at the ones spiritual, humane, ontological-psychological, very valuable and useful resources mostly in organizations from the fields as social services, culture, education, health and social care, etc.

The manager, strategist, supervisor engaged in leadership, planning, monitoring and mentoring activities, are useful, especially, qualities such as personal development (Lilienthal, 1967), humane development and humanity. The humane development and humanity anyway encompasses also the others, and gives to manager's personality and behavior those characteristics which help to operate both with the soul and with the mind.

From this point of view, the humanistic manager is a model and source of education and humane development of the professionals whom they coordinate, his personality is itself key-factor and source for personality and behavior development of the professionals from the organization.

To this end, the manager's personality must be described through higher qualifications of composition, structure and development (Kadushin & Harkness, 2014). The spiritual and moral sphere have high levels of development and dominant weight in the overall personality structure and composition, in the context of a very high moral and professional conscience, of a humanistic strong structured character, prosocial oriented.

Also, the manager, in humanistic management practice, is a humanist intellectual with vast and profound anthropological, philosophical, psychological, pedagogical, sociological, theological knowledge, the values and methods that promotes it relying on a good knowledge of the human, social phenomena, of the man in general also as a person, as individual, of the human rights culture (von Kimakowitz, Spitzeck, Pirson, Dierksmeier, Amann, 2011).

6.6. The Humanistic Managerial Practice

The humanistic managerial practice brings in the forefront of the leadership process concepts and ideas such as:

- responsibility for the employee's good, career and personal fulfillment;
- the employee as unicity;
- focus on the particular aspects of the organization;
- tolerance and attachment;
- employee-centered approach;
- the power/ force of the employee's personality, and consciousness;
- strength-based leadership;
- culture and spirituality;
- psychological-personal development;
- optimism;
- creativity;
- happiness;

- socio-human and professional accomplishment, etc. (von Kimakowitz, Spitzeck, Pirson, Dierksmeier, Amann, 2011).

The humanistic managerial act has, inter alia, the task, to operate/ determine those socio-humane improvements at the level of inter-personal relationship, group, organization that would lead, through the humanising force that exercise the socio-human/ humane relationships and the humanistic group upon the employee, to beneficial improvements in its psychological-professional activity/ effectiveness.

Therefore, based on the theoretical, axiological and teleological framework of the humanistic management, besides the universal tasks and activities, the role of the manager is to guide, help, educate, monitor, control, check the professionals' activity so that these ones to can contribute at the fulfilling the assumed organizational's mission.

In this end, the humanistic manager, must to work, with his knowledge, experience, soul and personality, at the formation and development of the professional and humane personality of the workers, of his professional attitudes and behavior, expressed in qualities of personality and conduct as conscientiousness, accountability, empathy/ compathy, agreeableness, happiness, personal/ human development, altruism, optimism, tolerance, etc.

Only to the extent that the subordinates professionals will acquire/ develop these traits and behaviors, as a result of the humanistic management activity, the manager may considers performing his managerial-formative task. The aspect highlighting the crucial educative dimension of the management in humanistic management, the essential rol that the manager plays, not only as a simple coordinator but rather as a man with a big heart, developed moral personality, as a model, as an educator, as a great character (von Kimakowitz, Spitzeck, Pirson, Dierksmeier & Amann, 2011).

6.7. People-Centered Management

People-Centered Management is conceived and is used especially from an existential and holistic perspective focusing, mostly on aspects, objectives and approaches such as:

- the manager must manifest increased trust in the employee's potential and creativity;

- the employee as being, subject, self matter and prevail in the relationships with the organization as a whole and with the economical goals;

- the manager experiences an empathetic understanding of the employee's personality and its personal/ social situation/ problems;

- the organizational/ professional relationship must be a relationship in which each person's perception of the other is very important;

- the employee must be involved in the organizational processes with all his psychological-personal and organizational/ professional experiences:

- the manager must to contribute at the solving of the employee's personal (psychological, familial, social) problems, challenges:

- The manager induces a sense of freedom and mutual responsibility in organization, etc. (F. Znaniecki, 1969; von Kimakowitz, Spitzeck, Pirson, Dierksmeier, Amann, 2011).

This kind of management approaches the organization as a socio-human whole, focusing on the concrete organizational socio-human situation, on the concrete, unique, existential organizational contexts using a phenomenological approach on the managerial act and process, involving the employee's inner psychological-personal, volitional capacities and aspirations, but simultaneously accepting its limitations and weaknesses.

One of the most important goal of the manager in the people-centered management is that to determine the employee to find and/or build professional meaning and purpose in their personal/ social life.

6.8. The Humanistic Approach in Art

The humanistic perspective brings in art the special interest and the focus on the complex human and spiritual world of emotions, passions, feeling, desires, incorporated in performances from art domains as theatre, film, literature, sculpture, picture, etc. (H. Khatchadourian, 1980)

In this sense, the humanistic approach in art research but also tries to incorporate in the artistic endeavor the resources of humane and spiritual personality, the resources and the qualities of the humane relationships/ coexistence, associated to the great human existential and ancestral aspiration to freedom, nondiscrimination, social justice, etc.

This perspective upon the art promotes, especially in literature, theatre and film, themes as:

- how humans specifically live, love, suffer, interact;

- the human relationships of kinship, friendship, enmity, interest, collegiality, power relationships;

- the resilience and coping with difficult situations;

- how persons and groups solve the problems;

- how persons and groups adapt to the changes or react to crisis or major events, etc. (J. Heilpern, 2000; Helbo, 1987).

6.9. Humanistic Aesthetics and Humanistic Theatrology

In the simplest sense, the science of art, *aesthetics* can be generally represented, implicitly or explicitly, directly or indirectly, as the scientifical-epistemological discipline, theoretical and practical area that researches and theorizes the art and the artist, reflected in a complex manner, incorporating, therefore, knowledge, ideas, theories, both from the philosophy of art but also from science (sociology, psychology, philosophy, anthropology, etc), developing, therefore, a multidisciplinary and interdisciplinary perspective on the artistic phenomenon, performance, on the artist, etc. (Helbo, 1987).

Going forward, **Humanistic Aesthetics** can be represented as the theoretical domain that researches and theorizes the art and the artist, reflected in a humanistic/ humane, complex and ideothetical/ existential manner, incorporating knowledge, ideas, theories, therefore, from the humanistic-existentialist sphere of thought and culture, from the humanistic psychology, humanistic sociology, and other sciences and practices of humanistic/ humane orientation, developing, consequently, a multi-disciplinary, inter-disciplinary, profound and spiritual perspective on the artistic phenomenon, on the performance, on the artist, on the artist's personality and the act of creation.

Humanistic Theatrology is interested especially of the emotional, socio-human, psychological-subjective, inter-personal, inter-human, inter-psychological processes, the concrete relationships and interpersonal phenomena and processes of influence, persuasion, knowledge (social perception and representation), cooperation and conflict, attachment and love, etc., involved in the process of elaboration and in the theatrical performance.

From the humanistic perspective on personality central roles in aesthetics (and theatrology), in art (theatre), in the act of creation and performance, in the theoretical representation of the artist, acquire the *humane* personality and the humane/ spiritual development, with the resources and features that they generate for all the people involved in the artistic phenomena, namely spirituality, altruism, agreeability, empathy, soulful welfare, sensitivity, authentic happiness, humanism, idealism, social solidarity, opposite but also complementary to the structural-functionalist, instrumental-behaviorist, and materialist model on the artist, or based mainly on so-called *personal (egotistical) development*, where central roles have the self/ ego, conscience, intelligence, will, or the professional competences, causing traits such as high self-control, high degree of awareness, of knowledge of self, high self-esteem, realism and balance, will development, resistance to failure and frustration, professional development, adaptability, individualism, materialism, hedonism, etc.

So, applied to the artistic field, to art, to theater in this case, to which we refer especially in this section, the humanistic paradigm, would brings into focus themes, issues such as:

- humanistic/ human source and explanation of the artist (actor)'s talent and personality;
- the humanistic concept of artistic personality, humane and spiritual structure of the artistic personality;
- humanistic representation and definition of the character (role);
- socio-humane relationships between the characters, and between the actors;
- compathtetic community of characters, artists, etc;
- humanistic screenplay and directing;
- humanistic spectacle;
- humanistic spectator;
- the humanistic mission of the artistic act, etc. (Helbo, 1987; H. Khatchadourian, 1980).

The theoretical framework that supports valorizes or rehabilitates the ontological-spiritual sphere of the person, of the humane personality in art (theater) could not therefore be than the one of the **humanistic aesthetics (theatrology)**.

6.10. The Character (Personage), the Artist and the Artistic Personality

To a great extent, the humanistic aesthetics and the humanistic theatrology must, somehow, to opposes to the structuralist-sociologist, behaviorist, and neuro-cybernetical representation of the person (interpreter/ actor, character, spectator, etc.) and the scenic compathetic community, and to propose a humanistic model, both as simple theoretical representation, and also as artistic/ anthropological ideal.

In theatrology, if in the structural-functionalist or cybernetic-scientistic paradigm/ model, the **character (personage)** is nomologically represented, as an individual, as an element in the social machinery, subjected to the universal structures and to the processes of group, community, society, etc, placing in the background its subjectivity, ego, soul, the particular ontology as existence, as being, as uniqueness, as destiny, instead the humanistic theatrology (especially the ontological-spiritual orientation) bring them in the spotlight, articulating a model of character of humanistic and spiritual type, and, through the force of the artistic induction, promoting, at the spectator level, a superior humane and spiritual model of man and community, responding thus at the implicitly humanistic mission of the theater.

Regarding the **interpreter's personality**, the interpreter's artistic personality, of the participant at the theatrical act, in the perspective of an authentic humanistic aesthetics and theatrology, these (the interpreter's personality, the interpreter's artistic personality) must to be highly developed - from the artistic-humanistic point of view, through all its spheres and sides: psychological, ontological, moral, etc., being necessary, to this end, to prioritizes the development of these spiritual, humane fields and instances of the artist's personality, expressed through traits, talents, humane behaviors such as empathy/ compathy, agreeability, dedication, humanism, sensitivity and spiritual development, virtue, charisma and others, generated, largely, of the existence and manifestation of the humane soul and the spiritual soul; of course on the background and in the context of the global spiritual development, in the context of the overall personal, humane and artistic development ((J. Heilpern, 2000; Helbo, 1987).

The art, especially the theater, through characters (personages), dramatic situations, difficult situations, conflicts, feelings, passions, feelings, heroes, tragedies reflects the dramatic and tragic, but also, sublime complexity of the socio-human existence.

In this sense only the artists (performers, directors, writers etc.) which incorporate in their **artistic personalities** and conducts the ontological and psychological complexity of the ancestral, historical, spiritual, cultural human being can bring, simulate, live these on the stage, in performance, can bring these from the reality, society, history or elsewhere in the face of the spectators.

It is the just reason that for the necessity of a powerful humanistic aesthetics and theatrology, constituted especially with the theoretical, scientific contribution of the humanistic psychology and humanistic sociology.

6.11. The Scenic Humane Community, the Humanist Director and the Humanistic Message

In humanistic theatrology any theatre scene is firstly an inter-human, inter-personalities, humane community. The knowledge of this aspect by the directors, playwrights, producers, actors, by all the persons and factors involved in the theatrical process and performance is a necessity.

The scenic humane community is build and specifically define through the common, collective, inter-/ trans-personal emotional, affective, sentimental, cognitive circumstances, characteristics and behaviors of the actors which play on scene.

It consists mainly of three types of psychological, psychosocial and humane scenic sub-processes or phenomena:

- emotional/ affective/ sentimental,

- cognitive/ intellectual, and

- spiritual/ cultural/ moral.

In this perspective each actor (character) of a Scenic humane community, is, inter alia, a product of a unique but also of a common, collective interaction, depending on the personalities involved in the theatrical act. Every actor being actually part of a particular socio-human system. This is, in turn, part of a comprehensive system.

Into any theatrical scene the humane valence and consistency is given by the fact that the involved actors' personalities are composed of common emotional, cognitive, and cultural experiences, by the fact that in each individual personality exists, through empathy and projection, the others. It is so established a mutual existential dependence between the actors and between the actors as individuals/ personalities and the scenic community as a whole (H. Khatchadourian, 1980).

The capitalization of the resources from the humane-scenic community, from the level and sphere of every participant on the artistic act is one of the most important task of the director.

In this sense, the **humanist director** is not a simple dramatic technician but a creator and an active participant in the process of production (J. Heilpern, 2000). Operating into the sphere of social, simple interpersonal scenic-community the main purpose of its activity is that to transform it in scenic-*humane* community.

Its personality, its humane/ spiritual behavior and thought represents, for this purpose, the means, the essential professional resource that can facilitate this artistic transformation/ metamorphosis.

In this mission the humanist director make an "insertion", an involvement. with whole its self, soul, intellect and experience, in the complex assembly of the scenic relationships, connections, conflicts, attachments, inter-empathies, compathies, feelings, passions, loves, projects, dramas - its intervention aiming to transform, them, therefore by means of his theatrical knowledge, experiences, humane personality, soul, and psychological-spiritual qualities, in *humane-scenic* community, with essential role in transmitting **the humanistic messages** to spectators.

Instead of Conclusions

This section of the book contains, with aim of synthesis and conclusions, the introductory subchapters of the book

In this book **humanism** (as rational thinking, through science, especially the socio-human sciences, and the human artistic creativity and imagination), **ontology** (as fundamental and constitutional domain of philosophy that has in its center of interest the category of *being, the existence in-itself*), the **philosophy of man** and the **social philosophy** (as theoretical-philosophical disciplines that study and interpret the man/human and society in terms of ethical, metaphysical and ontological values and categories), **existentialism** and **phenomenology** (that promote the displacement of the interest from the abstract, metaphysical themes, toward the existential, phenomenological themes, toward the concrete, determined, existing, particular entities), the **human rights philosophy/movement** (where all human beings are considered to be born free and equal in dignity and rights), the **secular humanism** and the **"Humanist Manifesto"** (that promote, from an atheistic position, the better rational understanding of ourselves, of our history, our intellectual and artistic achievements), **postmodernism** and Transmodernism (where the social and human entities are considered to be very fluid, constantly in unpredictable changing) and the **oriental philosophies and practices** (where the aim of life is considered to be, principally, the inner fulfillment of the person) are considered as main *sources* and *models* of the humanistic approach and method in the socio-human sciences and practices, of humanistic psychology and psychotherapy, of humanistic sociology and humanistic social work, of humanistic pedagogy and education, of humanistic management, of humanistic aesthetics.

In literature is considered that phenomenology and existentialism had and have central role in the imposition and maintaining of the humanistic approach in the socio-human sciences and practices, especially with their concerns for the displacement of the interest from the abstract, metaphysical themes toward the existential, phenomenological themes, the interest for the particular human condition and nature, the concrete, unique person-society relationship, the emphasis on real, lived life, the interest in topics such as happiness and distress, the limit experiences, the existential crises and impasses, the willpower and ability to self-determination, freedom and responsibility, the limits of the personal freedom, the ontological congruence between person and environment, the concrete social existence, from the speculative philosophy towards the philosophy of the concrete, determined, existing, particular man, the primacy of the man as an individual, person, ego, and uniqueness in society, the interest for personal growing and autonomy, the power of reason, the self-knowledge, the self-actualization, the self-realization, etc.

***

Essentially, the humanistic approach and method in the socio-human sciences and practices proposes, from the existential-positive position the representation of the person and personality through traits like high level of personal development, high capacity to self-determination, high resilience, high capacity to control the emotions, etc., and the socio-human micro-community through features such as strong organizational culture, high functionality, high cohesion, unity, solidity, adaptability, resilience, high autonomy, resistance to crisis and challenges, good management, etc., while from the ontological/spiritual (cultural) position it is highlighted especially the inner-ontological psychological-spiritual and psychological-humane content/ valence/ dimension of the personality, of the spiritual and humane self, and the inter-personal relationships of attachment, love, respect, the dominance of the practices and customs of mutual helps in community.

In the humanistic practices and researches the *analytic-inductive methods* are the principal scientific-methodological tools. This method may combines the rigor with the complexity, the general with the particular, leading to more relevant and useful results for the specific characteristics of the social and human phenomena and processes, taking both from the rigor of the quantitative techniques but also from the deepness, flexibility and comprehensivity of the qualitative techniques.

The specifics of the qualitative, interpretative and comprehensive methods in the socio-human sciences and practices is mainly that it focuses largely on capturing the *phenomena* more than the essences, the universal laws; the object of evaluation, observation and investigation being most often the event, the socio-human context, the sentiment, the concrete attitudes, feelings and reactions of people being in determined social and human relationships and processes.

The advantage is that through this approach is obtained the access to social and human aspects which would escape to an eminently nomological, scientific-technical approach, more focused on capturing the structural, universal and repeatable evidences.

✱✱✱

Psychology and psychotherapy has experienced in the second half of the twentieth century radical changes, in a large extent determined by the offensive of so-called *humanistic theory and method* in all the areas of the social sciences and practices.

With old origins even in antiquity, passing through Renaissance, and then reinvigorated by phenomenology and existentialism, the humanistic thinking and method have manifested powerfully initially in psychology as theory, instituting the humanistic psychology and, consequently, in psychotherapy, as the third way alongside psychoanalysis and behaviorism, both in theory and practice.

Therefore, how psychotherapy is "alimented", theoretically-methodologically, largely, from psychology, as theory and science, inevitably, directly or indirectly, their humanistic values, theories and methodology have made the presence increasingly in practice, redimensioning and reforming them, gradually and subtly, almost entirely, the humanistic theory and methodology succeeded, so gradually, to make place in the psychotherapy's literature and practice through values, objectives and terms such as *self-actualization, empowerment, accountability, human and personal development, happiness, self-determination, client-centered intervention* etc., also to determine even a shift of emphasis to values and goals such as *client's empowerment, human rehabilitation/ development, happiness, personal development of the person/ client,* etc.

What particularizes the humanistic methodology, in addition to the system of specific theory and method, is the human/ humane/ spiritual and humanistic-positive system of values and resources, which must, ultimately, to generate *the change,* the empowerment, the human rehabilitation and the reintegration, promoting as resources and values, on the one hand the *human personality,* the person, the individuality, the self/ego, the soul, the character, the skills, the will and the conduct, of the client as well of the professional, and, on the other hand, especially in humanistic group therapy, the *human, inter-human, inter-personal relationships,* the human relations lesser understood as mere social relations and mostly as *humane* relationships, generators of empowerment, human-psychological, personal development and happiness - resources for whose use the therapists appeal to ways of empowerment such as the empathy, the inter-empathy, the transfer, the psycho-social influence, etc.

Personality, as core category, values and resource is addressed in this chapter of the book by the two cardinal guidelines of the humanistic theory, respectively *existential-positive* and *ontological-spiritual/ humane,* speaking, therefore, in humanistic-ontological perspective of *spiritual/ humane personality,* and, in existential-positive perspective of *strong* and *developed personality.* The resilience and the change being obtained by the mobilization, development and control of these resources in the therapeutic process.

Too, a core concept in humanistic psychology, as personality trait, as well of the humanistic psychotherapy as objective but also as resource is *Personal Development,* that in this chapter is approached in close relation to the concept of *Strong Personality,* implying features as personal and social efficiency, socio-emotional development, high control of emotions, emotional intelligence, realism and balance, powerful will, resistance to failure and frustrations, hope, orientation to future. positive attitude, optimism, active thinking, high degree of awareness, self-knowledge, self-esteem, professional development, personal and social autonomy, interpersonal development, mature personality, adaptability.

To achieve these objectives the humanistic psychotherapy operates mainly with therapeutic methods or modalities like person-centered psychotherapy/ counseling, existential psychotherapy/ counseling, gestalt therapy and group psychotherapy, transpersonal and spiritual psychotherapy, positive psychotherapy, and experiential psychotherapy.

One of the most important ways of intervention in humanistic psychotherapy is the emancipation, empowerment and development of the client through its (re-) spiritualization and humanization, through spiritual and human/ humane empowerment and development. Even if is a very complex and difficult endeavor, the humanization, spiritualization and humane-spiritual/cultural integration/ development of the person/ client is described by the therapists, for some categories of clients, as miraculous solutions for many kinds of problems, sufferings, deviances, etc.

Therefore, the epistemological foundation of the evaluation in humanistic psychotherapy is the representation of the client as *complex personality*. In humanistic therapy the practitioner, through *his* complex personality, contributes crucially to the achievement of the humanistic established objectives, mostly those relating to the personal and spiritual development of the client, the empowerment and autonomization, the social, socio-humane integration and adaptation in the community where the it lives.

Through his personality, behavior, creativity and empathy the humanistic therapist works at the construction of a new (psychological-personal) *modus vivendi*, of some new (socio-human) behaviors, even of a new personality, with *humanistic* (existential and spiritual) tools and methods.

To this end, the level of development of the spiritual-empathetic traits of the professional, in any philosophy or theoretical orientation, form, doctrine of therapy, represents essential predictors of effectiveness and fulfillment of the objectives, the more in humanistic therapy, where this quality/ resource of the professional exceeds the original psychosocial meaning, instituting so as a core value-resource of the efficiency in practice.

***

Like psychology sociology has experienced in the second half of the twentieth century radical changes, in a large extent determined by the offensive of so-called *humanistic theory and method* in all the areas of the social sciences and practices. In the context of offensive of phenomenology and existentialism the humanistic thinking and method have manifested also in sociology, and, consequently in social work, instituting humanistic social work, in management, instituting humanistic management, and in other domains of practice that are "alimented", theoretically-methodologically, from sociology as science of the social phenomena and processes.

The same as in psychology and psychotherapy, in sociology and social work were imposed the two major orientations of the humanistic approach: *existential/ positive* and *ontological-cultural/ spiritual.*

Essentially, **the humanistic-existential (positive) direction/ theory** represents the socio-human (micro-) community through features such as strong organizational culture, high functionality, high cohesion, unity, solidity, adaptability, resilience, high autonomy, resistance to crisis and challenges, good management, etc., while **the humanistic-ontological-cultural/ spiritual approach/ theory** of community highlights ideas and features as people-centered community, dominance of the inter-personal relationships of attachment, love, respect, dominance of the practices and customs of mutual helps, social/ group/ community solidarity, harmony, unity, inter-personal congruency, socio-human, inter-personal, community functionality, socio-human, moral and cultural integration/ cohesion, the presence/ dominance of people with personality and behavior traits like altruism, empathy, kindness, goodness, tolerance, understanding, charity, helpfulness etc.

Crucial concept, value and objective in sociology and social work is **community development**, reveled of features such as social and economical efficiency, high control of the processes and activities, resistance to crisis, orientation to the future.

optimism, economic development, cultural development, institutional development, high autonomy, interpersonal development, high functionality, inter-community development, planning, collaboration, solidarity, democracy etc.

The humanistic-therapeutic/ assistential perspective on community, on the socio-human entities, promotes, therefore, a concept of community development where it is aimed to empower groups of people and the individuals with the skills they need to determine beneficial changes within their communities. These skills are often created through the formation of communities working for common goals.

Of the humanistic perspective, the great inclusive, cohesive, autonomous and developed communities incorporate, in a sublime manner, both the features of the organizational/ institutional development and the features of the humane, moral and cultural development, representing, in this connection, also, great values and resources in humanistic social work.

✸✸✸

In great measure, the humanistic paradigm of pedagogy and education is a replica of the humanistic paradigm of psychology and psychotherapy, the humanistic psychological theory and methodology succeeded, gradually, to make place in the pedagogy's literature and educational practice through values, objectives and terms such as *human and personal development, happiness, self-determination, person/child-centered education, positive education* etc., also to determine even a shift of emphasis to humanistic and positive values and goals of the education as institution.

Personality, as core category, values, objective and resource in humanistic pedagogy and education is addressed in this chapter of the book by the two cardinal guidelines of the humanistic theory/ approach, respectively *existential-positive* and *ontological-spiritual/humane*, speaking, therefore, in the humanistic-ontological perspective of *spiritual/ humane personality,* and, in existential-positive perspective of *strong* and *developed personality.* The education, personal development, professional and social formation and development, core objectives in humanistic education, being obtained by the mobilization, development and control of these resources in the educational process.

Essentially, the humanistic paradigm of education as process and activity brings in the forefront concepts and ideas such as child/student-centered approach, self-determination, self-actualization, the power/force of the ego, personality, consciousness, strength-based education/teaching, spirituality, empowerment, personal development, personal accomplishment, holistic assessment and teaching, optimism, creativity, happiness, the child's uniqueness, focus on the particular aspects of its human coexistence, tolerance, love, etc.

From a humanistic-positive position it is highlighted the importance in the educational process/ activity of some issues and resources as the strengths, the virtues, the talents of the child/ student, its positive experiences of learning, the positive relationships, happiness, the states of pleasure or flow, the positive emotions, the orientation of the learning to future, the positive expectations, appreciations, etc.

Essentially, the humanistic and positive pedagogies promote especially the formation, in the educational process, of the personality, of the person as a whole, as person in socio-human context, putting the objectives which aim the intellectual formation in second plan, yet without disregarding them. That is the reason way in process are used operational objectives as personality formation, personality development, personality empowerment, self-realization, psychological-personal development and empowerment, the humanization and spiritualization of the child/ student.

The existential directions/ modalities/ approaches focuses on the inner capacity of self-determination and formation of the child's personality, based on free will and self-realization, while the spiritual (humane, ontological, etc.) approaches focus on the formation, through education, of the child/ student as spiritual and humane personality.

In general, the humanistic approach in pedagogy and education prioritizes the role of some formative factors such as the human/humane quality of the adults' personalities, of the social, interpersonal, relationships, crucial role having in this sense the human quality of the learning community. Here we consider mainly the family and the school class, but also the communities of friends, neighbors, relatives etc. Both the family and the school class must be represented more than mere social groups, but especially like human/humane, spiritual, cultural, compathetic communities, that have essential contributions especially in the formation of social personality, core objective in humanistic education.

The humanistic perspective on the parent/teacher operates with a concept of professional personality of humane-spiritual type, which combines, dialectically, the humane and spiritual dimension with the one pragmatic. Empathy, spiritual welfare, humane and personal development and spiritual sensibility are crucial, indispensable traits of the teacher in humanistic pedagogy. These crucial interpersonal qualities and resources, involved in the educational process, have, mainly, as psychological-ontological source, its humane and spiritual personality, but also its strong personality.

The teacher/adult's personality is important especially in the educational objectives that involve the personal and human empowerment/development/formation. The theories of personality (development) describe and approach the child/student as *human being* situated in *process* of psychological, human, emotional and social development, where the adults' personalities have great contributions.

In this sense, crucial resources of education promoted by the humanistic pedagogy are empathy, happiness and love (attachment), being used as formative instruments, ways by the educators in achieving objectives as psychological-human and social-personal development, the educator-child educational relationship being in fact a framework for transfer humanity and spirituality, a subtle lane that the educator uses, intentionally and professionally, to achieve the assumed educational goals.

✱✱✱

Like sociology and psychology the managerial science and practice has experienced in the second half of the twentieth century radical changes, in a large extent determined by the offensive the humanistic theory and method in all the areas of the social sciences and practices. In the context of the offensive of the humanistic sociology and psychology, the humanistic theory and methodology have manifested gradually also in management, instituting the humanistic management, but also in other domains linked theoretically to sociology, including in art and aesthetics, instituting also humanistic aesthetics.

Essentially, the **humanistic approach to management** is guided by ideas, principles, values and objectives as: the manager must manifest increased trust in the employee's potential and creativity, the employee as being, subject, self, ego matter and prevail in the relationships with the organization as a whole and with the economical goals, the manager experiences an empathetic understanding of the employee's personality and personal/ social situation/ problems, the organizational/ professional relationship must be a relationship in which each person's perception of the other is very important, the employee must be involved in the organizational processes with all his psychological-personal and organizational/ professional experiences, the manager must to contribute to the solving of the employee's personal (psychological, familial, social) problems, challenges, the manager induces a sense of freedom and mutual responsibility in organization, etc.

In **art** the **humanistic approach** is focused on ideas, aspects and goals as: the humanistic/ humane source and explanation of the artist's talent and personality, the humanistic concept of artistic personality, the humane and spiritual structure of the artistic personality, the humanistic representation and definition of the character (personage), the socio-human/ humane relationships between the characters, but also between the artists, the compathtetic community of characters, artists, etc., the humanistic screenplay and directing, the humanistic spectacle, the humanistic mission of the artistic act, etc.

References
and Works Consulted

Adams, E.M. (1997), *A Society Fit for Human Beings* (S U N Y Series in Constructive Postmodern Thought), State University of New York Press.

Ainsworth, M.D.S., Blehar, M.C., Waters, E., Wall, S. (1978), *Patterns of Attachment: A Psychological Study of the Strange Situation*. Hillsdale, NJ: Lawrence Erlbaum Associates.

Allan, J., Pease, B, Briskman L. (2003), *Critical social work*, Melbourne: Allen & Unwin.

Allport, G.W. (1961), *Pattern and growth in personality*, New York: Holt, Rinehart &. Winston.

Allport, G. W (1985), *The historical background of social psychology*. In Lindzey, G; Aronson, E. The Handbook of Social Psychology. New York: McGraw Hill.

American Humane Association (2004), *Helping in Child Protective Services: A Competency-Based Casework Handbook*, Oxford University Press.

Anderson, R. (2011), *Transforming Self and Others through Research: Transpersonal Research Methods and Skills for the Human Sciences and Humanities* (SUNY Series in Transpersonal and Humanistic Psychology), SUNY Press

Andrieux, C. (1973), Perspectives nouvelles de recherche en personnologie. In: *L'année psychologique*. vol. 73, n°2. pp. 681-707.

Antony, M. (2008), *Shyness and Social Anxiety Workbook: Proven, Step-by-Step Techniques for Overcoming your Fear Pape*, Second Edition, New Harbinger Publications.

Aristotle, Robinson, D.N. (1999), *Aristotle's Psychology*, POLOS Ltd.

Arnet, J.J. (2011), *Human Development: A Cultural Approach*, Pearson.

Arts, W., Muffels, R., Meulen, R. (2001), *Solidarity in Health and Social Care in Europe* (Philosophy and Medicine), Kluwer Academic Publisher.

Bailey, R., Brake, M. (1975). *Radical Social Work*, Pantheon Books.

Barlow, D.H. (2007), *Clinical Handbook of Psychological Disorders*, Fourth Edition: A Step-by-Step Treatment Manual (Barlow: Clinical Handbook of Psychological Disorders), The Guilford Press.

Bandura, A. (1975), *Social Learning & Personality Development*, NY: Holt, Rinehart & Winston, INC.

Bandura, A., Locke, A. E. (2003), Negative self-efficacy and goal effects revisited. *Journal of Applied Psychology.*

Barbara, M.H. (2012), *Emergence: The Shift from Ego to Essence*, Hampton Roads Publishing.

Barrick, M. R., & Mount, M. K. (1991.) The Big Five personality dimensions and job performance: A meta-analysis. *Personnel Psychology*, 44, 1-26.

Batson, C.D. (2011), *Altruism in Humans*. New York: Oxford University Press.

Beaumont, H., Cobb Jr., J.B. (2012), *Toward a Spiritual Psychotherapy: Soul as a Dimension of Experience*, North Atlantic Books.

Beck, U. (1992), *Risk Society - Towards a New Modernity*, London: Sage.

Benner , D.G. (2011), *Soulful Spirituality: Becoming Fully Alive and Deeply Human*, Brazos Press (March.

Bellinger A, Elliott T. (2011), *What are you looking at? The potential of appreciative inquiry as a research approach for social work*. British Journal of Social Work 41: 708–725.

Bem, D (1970), *Beliefs, attitudes, and human affairs*. Belmont, CA: Brooks/Cole.

Berger, P.L. (1963), *Invitation to Sociology: A Humanistic Perspective*, NY: Anchor Books.

Berger, P.L., Luckmann, T. (1967), *The Social Construction of Reality: A Treatise in the Sociology of Knowledge*, Anchor.

Bergin, A.E. (2003), *Casebook for a Spiritual Strategy in Counseling and Psychotherapy*, Amer Psychological Assn.

Bergson, H. (2007), *Mind-Energy* ,Palgrave Macmillan.

Berkowitz, N. (1996), *Humanistic Approaches to Health Care: Focus on Social Work (Social Work in a Changing World)*, Venture Press.

Bertalanffy, L (1968), *General system theory: foundations, development applications*. New York: George Braziller.

Bickhard, M.H. (2012), The emergent ontology of persons. In: Jack Martin and Mark H. Bickhard (eds.) *The Psychology of Personhood*. pp. 165-180.

Biestek, F.P, Gehrig, C.C. (1978), *Client Self-Determination in Social Work*, Loyola Press.

Boudon., R. (1971), *La crise de la sociologie*, Geneve: Droz.

Bounds, M. (2010), *Welfare Policy: Feminist Critiques*, Wipf & Stock Pub.

Bowling, D., Ho attachments ffman, D. (2003), *Bringing Peace Into the Room: How the Personal Qualities of the Mediator Impact the Process of Conflict Resolution*, Jossey-Bass.

Bowlby J. (1999), *Attachment. Attachment and Loss* (vol. 1) (2nd ed.), New York: Basic Books.R. Brown.

Bradford, D.L., Burke, W.W. (2005), *Organization Development*, San Francisco: Pfeiffer.

Briar, S., Miller, H. (1971), *Problems and Issues in Social Casework*, New York: Columbia University Press.

Buechler, S.M. (2008), *Critical Sociology,* Paradigm Publishers.

Bugental, J. F. T. (1964), The third force in psychology. Journal of Humanistic Psychology, 4(1), 19–26.

Burkitt, I. (1991), *Social selves: Theories of the social formation of personality*, Sage Publications, London.

Byers, S.C. (2012), Perception, Sensibility, and Moral Motivation in Augustine: A Stoic-Platonic Synthesis, Cambridge University Press.

Bywater, I. (2010), *Aristotelis Ethica Nicomachea* (Cambridge Library Collection - Classics) (Ancient Greek Edition), Cambridge University Press.

Campbell-Sills, L., Cohan, S.L., & Stein, M.B. (2006), Relationship of resilience to personality, coping, and psychiatric symptoms in young adults, *Behaviour Research and Therapy*, 44 (4), 585-599.

Canda, E.R., Furman, L.D. (2009), *Spiritual Diversity in Social Work Practice: The Heart of Helping*, Oxford University Press.

Carlo, G., Eisenberg, N., Troyer, D., Switzer, G., & Speer, A. L. (1991), The altruistic personality: In what contexts is it apparent? *Journal of Personality and Social Psychology*, 450-458.

Chardin, P.T (1959), *The phenomenon of man*, New York: Harper and Row.

Chansky, T.E. (2008), *Freeing Your Child from Negative Thinking: Powerful, Practical Strategies to Build a Lifetime of Resilience, Flexibility, and Happiness*, Da Capo Lifelong Books.

Chelf, C.P. (1992), *Controversial Issues in Social Welfare Policy: Government and the Pursuit of Happiness (Controversial Issues in Public Policy)*, SAGE Publications, Inc.

Cicchetti, D., Carlson, V. (1989), *Child Maltreatment: Theory and Research on the Causes and Consequences of Child Abuse and Neglect*, Cambridge University Press.

Cloke C., Davies M. (1995), *Participation and empowerment in Chid Protection*, London, Pitman.

Cojocaru, S. (2013), *Appreciative Inquiry in Social Work: Theories and practices*, LAP LAMBERT Academic Publishing.

Coleman, C. (1998), *The Volunteer*, Grand Central Publishing.

Collins, D., Jordan, C., Coleman, H. (2010), *An Introduction to Family Social Work*, Belmont, Brooks/Cole.

Connor-Smith, J., & Flachsbart, C. (2007,) Relations between personality and coping: A meta-analysis. *Journal of Personality and Social Psychology*, 93, 1080-1107. doi:10.1037/0022-3514.93.6.1080.

Comte, A. (2004), *Catéchisme positiviste ou Sommaire exposition de la religion universelle*, Kindle Edition, EbooksLib.

Corey, G. (2012), *Theory and Practice of Counseling and Psychotherapy*, Cengage Learning.

Cortright, B. (1997), *Psychotherapy and spirit: Theory and practice in transpersonal psychotherapy*. Albany: State University of New York Press.

Cross, M.C. (2001), *Becoming a Therapist: A Manual for Personal and Professional Development*, Routledge.

Cuin, C.H. (2006), The nomologic approach in sociology, *Revue suisse de sociologie*, Switzerland, Seismo Verlag.

Cummins, K., Sevel, J.A., Pedrick, L. (2011), *Social Work Skills for Beginning Direct Practice: Text, Workbook, and Interactive Web Based Case Studies,* (3rd Edition), Pearson.

Cusick, A. (2011), *The Psychology of the Soul,* CreateSpace, Charleston SC, an Amazon.com Company.

Danesh, H.B. (1994), *Psychology of Spirituality,* Paradigm Publishing.

Denzin, N. K, Lincoln, Y. S. (2005), *The Sage Handbook of Qualitative Research* (3rd ed.), Thousand Oaks, CA: Sage.

DeVries, R., Zan, B. (2012), *Moral Classrooms, Moral Children: Creating a Constructivist Atmosphere in Early Education,* Teachers College Press.

Deurzen, E., Kenward, R. (2005), *Dictionary of Existential Psychotherapy and Counselling.* SAGE Publications.

Doherty, W.J. (1996), *Soul Searching: Why Psychotherapy Must Promote Moral Responsibility,* Basic Books.

Dominelli, L., Mc Leod, E. (1989), *Feminist Social Work,* MacMillian Press Ltd.

Dominelli, L. (2002), *Anti-Oppressive Social Work Theory and Practice,* Palgrave Macmillan.

Edwin, L. (2007), *Projective Psychology - Clinical Approaches To The Total Personality,* Pratt Press.

Elkin, D. (2009), *Humanistic Psychology: A Clinical Manifesto. A Critique of Clinical Psychology and the Need for Progressive Alternatives,* Universities of the Rockies Press.

Ellis, A. (1974), *Humanistic Psychotherapy: The Rational-Emotive Approach,* Mcgraw-Hill.

Ellenhorn, R. (1988), *Toward a Humanistic Social Work: Social Work for Conviviality,* New Jersey: Association for Humanist Sociology.

Ellis A., Abrams, M., Abrams, L.D. (2008), *Personality Theories: Critical Perspectives,* SAGE Publications, Inc.

Else, J.F. (1977), *Purposive social change: A radical humanist perspective,* Social Work Foundation, School of Social Work, University of Iowa.

Elson, M. (1988), *Self Psychology in Clinical Social Work,* W. W. Norton & Company.

Endler, N., Parker, J. (1992), Interactionism revisited: Reflections on the continuing crisis in the personality area, în *European Journal of Personality,* 6, pp. 177-198, http://www.ourfutureenvironment.org/personality/wp-content/uploads/2010/08/endler_ interactionism.pdf.

Erikson, E. H., Erikson, J.M. (1998), *The Life Cycle Completed* , W W Norton & Co Inc.

Feldman, R. (1985), Reliability and Justification, în *The Monist,* Buffalo, NY: Open Court Publishing Company.

Ferréol, G. (1998), *Dicţionar de sociologie,* Iaşi: Editura Polirom

Filip, J., McDaniel, N., Schene, P. (1999), *Helping in child protective services. A competency-based case-work handbook,* American Human Asociation, Englewood, Colorado.

Fox, P.J. (2011), *Heart of a Caregiver: Touching Lives with Compassion and Care,* Simple Truths.

Frankl, V. E. (1967), *Psychotherapy and existentialism: Selected papers on logotherapy,* New York: Simon and Schuster.

Freud, S., Strachey, J., Hitchens, C., Gay, P. (2010), *Civilization and Its Discontents* (Complete Psychological Works of Sigmund Freud), W. W. Norton & Company.

Friedman, H.S., Schustack, M.W. (2010), *Personality: Classic Theories and Modern Research* (5th Edition), Pearson.

Garfinkel, H. (2006), *Seeing sociologically,* Boulder, CO, Paradigm Publishers.

Game, A. (1991), *Undoing the Social: Towards a Deconstructive Sociology,* Toronto, University of Toronto Press.

Gammer, C. (2008), *The Child's Voice in Family Therapy: A Systemic Perspective,* W. W. Norton & Company.

Garrigou-Lagrange, R., Cummins, P. (1950), *Reality—A Synthesis Of Thomistic Thought,* St. Louis, Mo.: Herder.

Gerdes, K. E. Segal, E. A. (2009), A social work model of empathy. Advances in Social Work Practice, *Social Work* 10(2), 114-127.

Gerdes, K. E., Segal, E. A. (2011), The importance of empathy for social work practice: Integrating new science, *Social Work,* 56(2), 141-148.

Gerdes, K. E. (2011), Introduction: 21st century conceptualizations of empathy: Implications for social work practice and research, *Journal of Social Service Research,* 37(3), 226-229.

Gilgun, J.F. (2008), *The Four Cornerstones of Evidence-Based Practice in Social Work,* Jane Gilgun Books.

Gill, D.W. (2000), *Becoming Good: Building Moral Character*, IVP Books.

Gilligan, P. and Furness, S. (2006), *The Role of Religion and Spirituality in Social Work Practice: views and experiences of social workers and students*, British Journal of Social Work, 36 (4), 617 637.

Gill, M. (2011), Educating the Professional Social Worker: Challenges and Prospects, în *Revista de asistență socială*, nr. 4, pp. 30-41, Iași: Editura Polirom.

Ginsberg, L.H., Ginsberg, L. (2008), *Management and Leadership in Social Work Practice and Education*, Council on Social Work Education.

Gleick, J. (1987), *Chaos: Making a New Science*, Viking Press.

Goldstein, H. (1984), *Creative Change: A Cognitive-Humanistic Approach to Social Work Practice*, Routledge.

Goldstein, E.G. (1995), *Ego Psychology and Social Work Practice*: 2nd Edition, The Free Press.

Gonzalez-Mena, J. (2012), *Child, Family, and Community: Family-Centered Early Care and Education*, Pearson.

Goroff, N. (1981), *Humanism and Social Work Paradoxes*, Problems, and Promises, The Journal of Sociology & Social Welfare: Vol. 8: Iss. 1.

Grinnell Jr, R.M., Unrau, Y.A., (2010), *Social Work Research and Evaluation: Foundations of Evidence-Based Practice*, Oxford University Press.

Goodman, A. (1990), T*he Impact of Humanism on Western Europe.* Longman,

Hall, E., Hall C. (1988), *Human relations in education.* Psychology Press.

Hall, E. (1966), *The Hidden Dimension*, New York, Anchor Books.

Harel, I., Papert, S. (1991), *Constructionism,* Norwood, Ablex Publishing Corporation.

Hamblin, R. L., Buckholdt, D., Ferritor, D., Kozloff, M., Blackwell, L. (1971), *The Humanization Processes: A Social, Behavioral Analysis of Children's Problems*, Krieger Pub Co.

Hamilton, E., Cairns, H., Cooper, L. (2005), *The Collected Dialogues of Plato: Including the Letters,* Princeton University Press.

Hardcastle, A. (2011), *Theories and Skills for Social Workers,* 3 edition, Oxford University Press.

Harkness, D. (2002), *Supervision in Social Work,* Columbia University Press.

Healy, L. (2008), *International social work: Professional action in an interdependent world.* 2d ed. Oxford: Oxford Univ. Press.

Hegel, G.W.F. (1977), *Phenomenology of Spirit,* translated by A.V. Miller with an analysis of the text and foreword by J.N. Findlay. Oxford: Oxford University Press.

Heidegger, M. (1962), *Being and Time,* trans. J. Macquarrie and E. Robinson, San Francisco, CA: Harper &Row.

Habermas J., Lenhardt, C. (2001), *Moral Consciousness and Communicative Action,* The MIT Press.

Harvey, P. (1995), *The selfless mind: Personality, consciousness and Nirvana in early Buddhism.* Richmond, England: Curzon Press.

Helbo, A. (1987), *Theory of Performing Arts,* John Benjamins Publishing Company.

Heilpern, J. (2000), *How Good is David Mamet, Anyway: Writings on Theatre and Why it Matters,* New York: Routledge.

Hepworth, D. H. și al. (2009), *Direct Social Work Practice: Theory and Skills,* 8 edition Cengage Learning.

Hobson, J.A. (1933), *Rationalism and Humanism,* London: Watts & Co.

Hofweber, T. (2004), Logic and Ontology. In Zalta, Edward N. *Stanford Encyclopedia of Philosophy.*

Hoffman, M.L. (2000), *Empathy and moral development: Implications for caring and justice.* New York: Cambridge University Press.

Horner, N., Kindred, M. (1997), *Using Humanist/Existential Theories in Social Work (Using Theories in Social Work),* Open Learning Foundation.

Howe, D. (1995), *Attachment Theory for Social Work Practice,* Palgrave Macmillan.

Howe, D. (2009), *A Brief Introduction to Social Work Theory,* Palgrave Macmillan.

Hughes, D.A. (2000), *Facilitating Developmental Attachment: The Road to Emotional Recovery and Behavioral Change in Foster and Adopted Children,* Jason Aronson, Inc.

Humanistische Akademie. (1998). *Humanistische Sozialarbeit*, Berlin: Humanistische Akademie. Series: Humanismus aktuell, H. 3. Jg. 2.

Husserl, E., Moran D. (2012, *Ideas: General Introduction to Pure Phenomenology*, Routlege.

Ife, J. (2012), *Human Rights and Social Work: Towards Rights-Based Practice*, Cambridge University Press.

Illomen, K. (2011), *A Social and Economic Theory of Consumption*, Palgrave Macmillan.

Inderbitzin, M.L., Bates, C.A., Gainey, R.R. (2012), *Deviance and Social Control: A Sociological Perspective*, SAGE Publications.

James, W. (1981), *Pragmatism: A New Name for Some Old Ways of Thinking*, Hackett Publishing.

Jex, S.M., Gudanowski D.M. (1992), Efficacy beliefs and work stress: An exploratory study. *Journal of Organizational Behavior*.

Jones, C. (1993), *New Perspectives on the Welfare State in Europe*, London: Routledge.

Jung, C.G. (1981), *The Archetypes and The Collective Unconscious* (Collected Works of C.G. Jung Vol.9 Part 1), Princeton University Press.

Khatchadourian, H. (1980), Humanistic functions of the Arts today. *Journal of Aesthetic. Education*, 14(2), 11-22.

Kellerman, H. (2012), *Personality: How it forms*. New York: American Mental Health Foundation.

Kelly G.A. (1991), *The Psychology of Personal Constructs*, London: Routledge.

Kierkegaard, S. (1981), *The Concept of Anxiety: A Simple Psychologically Orienting Deliberation on the Dogmatic Issue of Hereditary Sin* (Kierkegaard's Writings, VIII) Princeton University Press.

Kimakowitz, E., Spitzeck, H., Pirson, M., Dierksmeier, C., Amann, W. (2011), *Humanistic Management in Practice*, Houndmills: Palgrave Macmillan

Kirsley, D. (2010), *Personology*, Prometheus Nemesis Book Company.

Koller, J. M. (1985), *Oriental Philosophies*. New York: Charles Schribner's Sons.

Kostelnik, M. (2011), *Guiding Children's Social Development and Learning (What's New in Early Childhood)*, Cengage Learning.

Kotarba, J.A., Johnson, J.M. (2002), *Postmodern existential sociology*, Walnut Creek, CA, Alta Mira.

Kreeft, P. (1992), *Back to Virtue: Traditional Moral Wisdom for Modern Moral Confusion*, Ignatius Press.

Krill, D.F. (1978), *Existential social work*, New York: Free Press,

Kramer-Moore, D., Moore, M. (2012), *Destructive Myths in Family Therapy: How to Overcome Barriers to Communication by Seeing and Saying -- A Humanistic Perspective*, Wiley-Blackwell.

Kroeber, A. L., Kluckhohn, C. (1952), *Culture: A Critical Review of Concepts and Definitions,* New York: Vintage Books.

Kurtz, P. (2006), *What is secular humanism?* Amherst, NY: Prometheus Books.

Lacan, J. (1991), *The Seminar of Jacques Lacan: Book II: The Ego in Freud's Theory and in the Technique of Psychoanalysis* , W. W. Norton & Company, 1991.

Lajoie, D. H. & Shapiro, S. I. (1992), Definitions of transpersonal psychology: The first twenty-three years. *Journal of Transpersonal Psychology*, Vol. 24.

Langan, T. (2009), *Human Being: A Philosophical Anthropology*, University of Missouri Press.

Lavalette, M. (ed.) (2011), *Radical Social Work Today: Social Work at the Crossroads*, Bristol: Policy Press.

Lazarus, R. S., (1961), *Adjustment and Personality*, New York: McGraw-Hill Book.

Ledwith, M. (2005), *Community development: A critical approach,* Bristol: The Policy Press.

Leight, A. K. (2001), Transpersonalism and social work practice: Awakening to new dimension for client self-determination, empowerment, and growth[A]. In E. R.Canda & E. D. Smith (ed.). *Transpersonal perspectives on spirituality in social work* (pp.63-76)[C]. New York: The Haworth Press, Inc.

Lerner, M. (2011), *Education And A Radical Humanism: Notes Toward A Theory Of The Educational Crisis,* Licensing, LLC.

Levi-Strauss, C. (1969), *The elementary structures of kinship*, Beacon Press, Boston.

Lietz, C. A. și al. (2011), The empathy assessment index (EAI): A confirmatory factor analysis of a five component model of empathy, *Journal of the Society for Social Work and Research*, 2(2), 104-124.

Lilienthal, D.E. (1967), *Management: A Humanist Art*, Carnegie Institute of Technology.

Lock, A., Strong, T. (2010), *Social constructionism: Sources and stirrings in theory and practice*, New York: Cambridge University Press.

Lukacs, G. (1978), *Ontology of Social Being*, Volume 1, Hegel, Merlin Press.

Madanes, C. (2006), *The Therapist as Humanist, Social Activist, and Systemic Thinker*, Zeig, Tucker & Theisen, Inc.

Maddi, S.R., Costa, O.T. (1972), *Humanism in Personology: Allport, Maslow, and Murray (Perspectives on personality)*, Aldine•Atherton.

Magee, L., James, P., Scerri, A. (2012), Measuring Social Sustainability: A Community-Centered Approach. *Applied Research in the Quality of Life* 7 (3): 239–61.

May, G.G. (1987), *Will and Spirit: A Contemplative Psychology*, HarperOne.

Mayo, E. (1933), *The human problems of an industrial civilization.* Cambridge, MA: Harvard.

Maslow, A.H. (1993), *The Farther Reaches of Human Nature*, Penguin / Arkana.

Maslow, A.H. (2011), *Toward A Psychology of Being* - Reprint of 1962 Edition, Martino Fine Books.

Masters, A., Wallace, H.R. (2010), *Development for Life and Work*, 10 edition, Cengage Learning.

Maritain, J. 1956), *Existence and the Existent: An Essay on Christian Existentialism*, trans. L. Galantiere and G.B. Phelan, New York: Image.

McAdams, D. P. (2009), *The person: An introduction to the science of personality psychology* (5th Ed.). New York: Wiley.

McBeath, G., & Webb, S. A. (2002). Virtue ethics and social work: Being lucky, realistic, and not doing one's duty. British Journal of Social Work, 32, 1015-1036.

Mc Call, L.A. (2001), *The McCall Body Balance Method : Simple Concepts for Ageless Movement*, Lisa Mccall.

McLaren, N. (2010), *Humanizing Psychiatrists: Toward a Humane Psychiatry*, Future Psychiatry Press.

Mead, M. (2001), *Coming of Age in Samoa: A Psychological Study of Primitive Youth for Western Civilisation* (Perennial Classics), William Morrow.

Merton, R. K., Nisbet, R. A. (Eds.). (1961), Contemporary Social Problems: An Introduction to the Sociology of Deviant Behavior and Social Disorganization. New York: Harcourt, Brace & World.

Mille, S. (2009), *The Moral Foundations of Social Institutions: A Philosophical Study,* Cambridge University Press.

Miller, J.P. (1999), *Education and the Soul: Toward a Spiritual Curriculum,* State University of New York Press.

Miller, J.P. (2005), *Holistic Learning And Spirituality In Education: Breaking New Ground,* State University of New York Press.

Million, T. (1990), *Toward a New Personology: An Evolutionary Model.* New York: Wiley.

Mills, C. W. (1959), *The sociological imagination,* Oxford University Press, London.

Minsky, M. (2007), *The Emotion Machine: Commonsense Thinking, Artificial Intelligence and the Future of the Human Mind,* Simon & Schuster.

Mjoset, L. (2009), The contextualist approch to social science Methodology, în David, B., Ragin, C.C. (coord), *The SAGE hanbook of case-based Methods,* London: SAGE Publication Ltd., pp. 39-68.

Moody R., Carroll, D. (1997), *The Five Stages of the Soul: Charting the Spiritual Passages That Shape Our Lives,* New York: Anchor Books.

Moghaddam, F.M. (1998), *Social psychology,* New York: W.H. Freeman end Company.

Molinari, C. (1998), The relationship of community quality to the health of women and men, *Social Science & Medicine,* 47(8), 1113—1120.

Montessori, M. (1968), *Formazione dell'uomo,* Garzanti, Milano.

Moore, T. (1994), *Care of the Soul : A Guide for Cultivating Depth and Sacredness in Everyday Life,* HarperPerennial.

Moore, T. (1994), *Soul Mates: Honoring the Mystery of Love and Relationship,* HarperPerennial.

Moustakas, C. (1966), *Existential Child Therapy,* Basic Books Inc.

Moustakas, C. (1994), *Phenomenological Research Methods,* Thousand Oaks, California: Sage Publications.

Mowrer, E.R. (1972), *Family Disorganization: An Introduction to a Sociological Analysis*, Arno Press and The New York Times.

Mullaly, B. (2006), *The New Structural Social Work: Ideology, Theory, Practice*, 3rd (third) Edition, Oxford University Press.

Mullaly, B. (2002), *Challenging Oppression: A Critical Social Work Approach*, Oxford University Press.

Murray, H. A. (2007). *Explorations in Personality*. Oxford University Press; 70th Anniversary Edition.

Myers, D. G. (2004), *Theories of Emotion. Psychology*: Seventh Edition, New York, NY: Worth Publishers.

Netting, F.E., Kettner, P.M., McMurtry, S.L., Thomas, M.L. (2011), *Social Work Macro Practice* (5th Edition), Pearson.

Noam, G.G., Wren, T.E. (1993), *Moral Self: Building a Better Paradigm*, The MIT Press.

Noddings, N. 2003, *Happiness and education*, Cambridge University Press.

Nolan, P., Lenski, G. (2010), *Human Societies: An Introduction to Macrosociology*, Oxford University Press.

O'Hare, T. (2005), *Evidence-Based Practices for Social Workers: An Interdisciplinary Approach*, Lyceum Books.

Outhwaite, W. (2006), *The Future of Society* (Blackwell Manifestos), Wiley-Blackwell.

Panter-Brick, C., Smith, M.T. (2000), *Abandoned Children*, Cambridge University Press.

Parsons, T. (1978), *Social Systems and the Evolution of Action Theory*, New York: Free Press.

Payne, M. (2011), *Humanistic Social Work. Core Principles in Practice*, Basingstoke, Hampshire, England: Palgrave Macmillan.

Payne, M. (2005), *Modern Social Work Theory*, Lyceum Books.

Patterson, C. H. (1973), Humanistic education, Englewood Prentice.

Pelzer, D. (1997), *The Lost Boy: A Foster Child's Search for the Love of a Family*, Health Communications.

Plato and Benjamin Jowett (2005), *Protagoras and Meno*, Penguin Classics.

Plotnik, R., Kouyoumdjian, H. (2007), *Introduction to Psychology*, Belmont: Wadsworth Publishing Company.

Pound, R. (1996), *Social Control through Law*, Transaction Publishers.

Punalekar, S.P. (1983), *Deprivation, institutionalisation and development: A study of child welfare institutions in Gujarat*, Centre for Social Studies.

Reamer, F. G. (1993), *The philosophical foundations of social work*, New York: Columbia University.

Reichmann, J. B. (1985), *Philosophy of the human person*. Chicago, Il.: Loyola University Press.

Reis, H. T., Collins, W. A., & Berscheid, E. (2000), The relationship context of human behavior and development. *Psychological Bulletin*, 126, 844-872.

Rickert, H. (1986), *The Limits of Concept Formation in Natural Science*, Cambridge University Press.

Rifkin, J. (2009), The *Empathic Civilization: The Race to Global Consciousness in a World in Crisis*, Tarcher.

Roberts, A.R., Yeager, KR. (2006), *Foundations of Evidence-Based Social Work Practice*, Oxford University Press.

Rogers, C. R. (1951), *Client-Centered Therapy: Its Current Practice, Implications, and Theory*, Boston: Houghton Mifflin.

Rogers, C.R. (1959), A Theory of Therapy, Personality and Interpersonal Relationships as Developed in the Client-centered Framework. In (ed.) S. Koch, *Psychology: A Study of a Science*, New York: McGraw Hill.

Rogers, C.R. (1977), *On Personal Power: Inner Strength and Its Revolutionary Impact*, Delacorte Press.

Rogers, C.R. (1980), *A Way of Being*, Boston: Houghton Mifflin

Ross, E.A. (2002), *Social Control: A Survey of the Foundations of Order*, University Press of the Pacific.

Rubin, A, Babbi, E.R. (2012), *Research Methods for Social Work*, Brooks/Cole Empowerment.

Rutter, S.M, Smith, D.J. (1995), *Psychosocial Disorders in Young People: Time Trends and Their Causes*, Wiley.

Sandu, A. (2013*), Social Work Practice: Research Techniques and Intervention Models: From Problem Solving to Appreciative Inquiry*, LAP LAMBERT Academic Publishing.

Saran, P. (1998), *Tantra: Hedonism in Indian Culture*, DK Printworld.

Schellhamme, E (2012), *Become a Strong Personality*, Charleston, SC: CreateSpace.

Schick, T. (Ed.). (1999), *Readings in the philosophy of science: From positivism to postmodernism.* New York: McGraw-Hill.

Schooler, J.E. (2010), *Wounded Children, Healing Homes: How Traumatized Children Impact Adoptive and Foster Families,* NavPress.

Schreurs, A. (2001), *Psychotherapy and Spirituality: Integrating the Spiritual Dimension into Therapeutic Practice,* Jessica Kingsley Pub.

Segal, E.A., Gerdes, K.E., Steiner, S. (2010), *An introduction to the profession of social work* (3rd ed.), Belmont, CA: Brooks/Cole.

Seidman, B.F. (2004), *Toward A New Political Humanism,* Prometheus Books.

Seligman, M.E., Csikszentmihalzi, P. (2000), Positive Pshyhology, în *American Psychologist,* vol. LV, nr. 1.

Seligman, M. E. P. (2002), *Authentic Happiness.* New York: Free Press.

Seligman, M., & Fowler, R. (2011), Comprehensive soldier fitness and the future of psychology, *American Psychologist.* 66.

Schutz A. (1972), *The Phenomenology of the Social World,* London: Heinemann Educational Books.

Shebib, B. (2002), *Choices: Counseling Skills for Social Workers and Other Professionals,* Pearson.

Shemmings, D. (2011), *Understanding Disorganized Attachment: Theory and Practice for Working With Children and Adults,* Jessica Kingsley.

Smith, D. (2004), *Social work and evidence based practice,* London: Jessica, Kingsley.

Smuts, J. C. (1973), *Holism and Evolution,* Westport. Connecticut: Greenwood Press.

Snyder, C.R. & Lopez, S.J. (2006), *Positive Psychology: The Scientific and Practical Explorations of Human Strengths,* Thousand Oaks, CA: Sage.

Sousa, D.A. (2010), *Mind, Brain and Education: Neuroscience Implications for the Classroom,* Hardcover Solution Tree.

Stairs, J. (2000), *Listening for the Soul: Pastoral Care and Spiritual Direction,* Fortress Press.

Stangor, C. (2004), *Social groups in action and interaction,* New York: Psychology Press.

Steiner, R. (1972), *A Modern Art of Education*. London: Rudolf Steiner Press.

Steiner, R. (1996), *The education of the child, and early lectures on education*, Hudson, N.Y.: Anthroposophic Press.

Stern, E.M., Kramer, S.Z. (1995), *Transforming the Inner and Outer Family: Humanistic and Spiritual Approaches to Mind-Body Systems Therapy*, Routledge.

Stolorow, R. D. (2011), Toward a renewal of personology in psychotherapy research, *Psychotherapy*, 442–444.

Stone, J.D. (1999), Soul Psychology: How to Clear Negative Emotions and Spiritualize Your Life, Wellspring/Ballantine.

Storr, A. (1992), *The Integrity of the Personality*, Ballantine Books.

Stefaroi, P. (2007), Efficient Management Particularity in Social Work), *Social Work Review*, No. 3, Polirom Publishing House.

Stefaroi, P. (2008), Socio-Affective Development Disorders of Institutionalized Child. From The Survival Objective towards the Happiness Objective in Social Work for Children, *Social Work Review*, No. 1-2, Polirom Publishing House.

Stefaroi, P. (2009), Humanistic Perspective on Customer in Social Work, *Social Work Review*, No. 1-2, Polirom Publishing House.

Stefaroi, P. (2009), *Happiness Theory in Social Work. From Care Management to Happiness Management)*, Lumen Publishing House.

Stefaroi, P. (2012), Humanistic Paradigm of Social Work or Brief Introduction in Humanistic Social Work, *Social Work Review*, No. 1, Polirom Publishing House.

Strack, S. (2005), *Handbook of Personology and Psychopathology*, Wiley.

Stemberger, G. (2008), Gestalt Theoretical Psychotherapy (GTP). In: H. Bartuska et al. (eds.), *Psychotherapeutic Diagnostics - Guidelines for the New Standard*, Vienna - New York: Springer.

Stets, J. E., Carter, M. J. (2011), The moral self: Applying identity theory. *Social Psychology Quarterly*, 74, 192–215.

Tiryakian, E.A. (1962), *Sociologism and existentialism, two perspectives on the individual and society*, Englewood Cliffs, N.J., Prentice-Hall.

Thomas, L. (2007), *Contemporary Debates in Social Philosophy*, Wiley-Blackwell.

Thomas, S.C. (1996), *A sociological perspective on contextualism,* în *Journal of Counseling and Development,* JCD, July 1, 74(6), 529-541, http://www.highbeam.com/doc/1P3-10006742.html.

Timberlake, E.M., Cutler, M.M. (2000), *Developmental Play Therapy in Clinical Social Work,* Pearson.

Tsui, M. (2004), *Social Work Supervision: Contexts and Concepts,* SAGE Publications.

Vanier, J. (1989), *Community and Growth,* New York: Paulist Press.

Vico, G. (1993), *On Humanistic Education: Six Inaugural Orations, 1699-1707 (Six Inaugural Orations, 1699-1707 : from the Definitive Latin Text, Introduction, and Notes of Gian Galeazzo Visconti),* Cornell University Press.

Vincent, J-D., Hughes, J. (1990), *The Biology of Emotions,* Blackwell Pub.

von Bertalanffy, L., (1968), *General System Theory. Foundations, Development, Applications.* Braziller, New York.

Von Kimakowitz, E., H. Spitzeck, M. Pirson, C. Dierksmeier, and W. Amann (eds.). (2011). *Humanistic management in practice.* New York: Palgrave Macmillan.

Walsh, M. (2006), *Nurse Practitioners: Clinical Skill and Professional Issues,* 2 edition, Butterworth-Heinemann.

Walsh, R, Vaughan, F. (1993), *Paths beyond Ego: The Transpersonal Vision,* Los Angeles, CA: J. Tarcher.

Wallace, A. F. C. (1980), Culture and Personality (2d ed.), New York: Random House.

Ward, C.C. (2010), *Strength-Centered Counseling: Integrating Postmodern Approaches and Skills With Practice,* SAGE Publications, Inc.

Watson, D., Clark, L. A., Tellegen, A. (1988), Development and validation of brief measures of positive affect and negative affect, în *Journal of Personality and Social Psychology,* Washington: American Psychological Association. Găsit la adresa http://www.apa.org/pubs/journals/psp/.

Watt, I. (1957), *The Rise of the Novel,* Berkeley, University of California.

Webb, N.B. (2005), *Working with Traumatized Youth in Child Welfare (Social Work Practice with Children and Families,* The Guilford Press.

Weissman, D. (2000), *A social ontology,* London: Yale University Press.

Weisman, C. S., Nathanson, C. A. (1985). Professional satisfaction and client outcomes: A comparative organizational analysis. *Medical Care*, 23, 1179–1192.

Wheeler, G. (1991), *Gestalt reconsidered*, New York: Gardner Press.

Whitaker, C. W. A. (2002), *Aristotle's De Interpretatione: Contradiction and Dialectic* (Oxford Aristotle Studies), Oxford University Press.

Williams, B. (1993), *Introducere în etică*, București: Editura Alternative.

Wilber, K. (2000), *Integral Psychology: Consciousness, Spirit, Psychology, Therapy*, Shambhala.

William K. F. (2012), *Opening to the Sacred: A Humanist Approach to Holistic Spirituality*, Premium Prose Publishing.

Wing Sue, D. (2006), *Multicultural social work practice*, USA: WILEY.

Whiteside, (1969), *Personology: The Dynamics of Success,* New York: F. Fell.

Wommack, A. (2010), *Spirit, Soul and Body*, Harrison House.

Yalom, I. (1980), *Existential psychotherapy*. New York: Basic Books.

Young, P.T. (1961), *Motivation and Emotion*, John Wiley & Sons Inc.

Zamfir. E. (2008), The new human model proposed by humanist pychology. Types of conflict resolution, in *Social Work Review*, nr. 1-2, pp 3-28.

Zastrow, Ch. (2009), *Introduction to Social Work and Social Welfare: Empowering People,* Thomson Brooks/Cole.

Zheng, R. (Ed.). (2012), *Evolving psychological and educational perspectives on cyber behavior*, Hershey.

Znaniecki, F. (1934) The method of sociology, New York: Farrar and Rinehart.

Znaniecki, F. (1969), *On humanistic sociology*, Chicago: University of Chicago Press.

*** www.books.google.ro/.

*** www.americanhumanist.org/humanism/ humanist_manifesto_iii

*** www.ifsw.org/.

*** www.ohchr.org/EN/UDHR.

*** www.scribd.com/.

*** www.un.org/en/documents/udhr/.

The Humanistic Approach in Psychology & Psychotherapy, Sociology & Social Work, Pedagogy & Education, Management and Art:

Personal Development and Community Development

by Petru Stefaroi

Available on Amazon.com, Amazon Europe, CreateSpace Store, and other retail outlets

---

CreateSpace

4900 LaCross Road

North Charleston, SC 29406

USA

http://www.amazon.com/
https://www.createspace.com/

Author's email address:

petrustefaroi@yahoo.com

The
Humanistic Approach
in
Psychology & Psychotherapy,
Sociology & Social Work,
Pedagogy & Education,
Management and Art:

Personal Development
and
Community Development